Soiled Doves

PROSTITUTION In The Early West

Other non-fiction books
by Anne Seagraves

Roses Of The West © 2002

Daughters of the West © 1996

High~Spirited Women Of The West © 1992

Women Who Charmed The West © 1991

Women Of The Sierra © 1990

Tahoe, Lake In The Sky © 1987

Beautiful Lake County © 1985

Soiled Doves

PROSTITUTION In The Early West

By Anne Seagraves

Published by WESANNE PUBLICATIONS
Post Office Box 428
Hayden, Idaho 83835

Library of Congress Number 93-94257
ISBN 0-9619088-4-X

ACKNOWLEDGMENTS

Amon Carter Museum, Fort Worth, TX; Arizona Historical Society, Tucson, AZ; California History Center, De Anza College, Cupertino, CA; California State Library, Sacramento, CA; Cheney Cowles Museum, Spokane, WA; Colorado Historical Society, Denver, CO; Idaho, University of, Moscow, ID; Kansas City Posse of Westerners, Kansas City, KS; Kansas State Historical Society, Topeka, KS; Lake County Museum, Lakeport, CA; Montana Historical Society, Helena, MT; Montana, University of, Missoula, MT; Nevada Historical Society, Reno, NV; Old Montana Bar & Grill, Saltese, MT; Panhandle Plains Historical Museum, Canyon, TX; Puget Sound Maritime Historical Society, Seattle, WA; Seattle Historical Society, Seattle, WA; Silver Bowl Archives, Butte, MT; Wallace Mining Museum, Wallace, ID; Washington, University of, Seattle, WA, and Wyoming State Museum, Cheyenne, WY.

In researching *Soiled Doves*, many individuals have been extremely helpful. The author would like to thank the following people:

Bob Clark, Montana Historical Society, Helena, MT; Jack Fiske, Tombstone, AZ; Douglas McDonald, Grantsdale, MT; Mark Pupich, State Ranger, Bodie State Historic Park, CA; Arlene Reveal, County Librarian, Bridgeport, CA, and Charles Mutschler, Assistant Archivist, Eastern Washington University, Cheney, WA.

AND A VERY SPECIAL THANK YOU TO: Helen Evans, for the use of her mother's book, *The Story of Bodie*, by Ella M. Cain, which made the Lottie Johl story possible; Timothy Gordon, Missoula, MT, for photos from his private collection and historical data; Jill Lachman, Hayward, CA, Photographer and seasonal aide at Bodie State Park; Deborah Mellon, Kellogg, ID, for sharing her book *The Legend of Molly b' Dam'*; Ben T. Traywick, Tombstone, AZ, for photos from his private collection and historical data; AND Betty Ruckhaber, Coeur d'Alene, ID, for her expert secretarial services; Valle Novak, Sandpoint, ID, for professional editing; Julie Knudsen, Graphic Artist, Sacramento, CA, for outstanding artwork throughout the book, and as always, to my husband, Wes, who has been with me every step of the way in the writing of this very difficult book.

Prostitution is considered to be either good or bad, depending upon how it is perceived by each society. It has been recorded as far back as the Sumerian Empire, in 2000 B.C., where a prostitute was respected as a temporary wife or companion.

Through the ages, the act of providing sex in return for favors or money has been an accepted way of life for many cultures. In the Old World, goddesses such as Aphrodite, the goddess of love and desire, and Ishtar, the goddess of fertility, were worshipped. Temple prostitutes held a place of honor. They entertained the rulers or visiting priests and donated the money back to the temples. The most beautiful were sacrificed to the gods.

Although most European countries had laws against prostitution during the 19th century, the police seldom bothered to enforce them. Many members of royalty kept one or several mistresses, but as a rule the regular ladies of the night were looked upon as objects of ridicule and scorn. Queen Victoria's strict morality temporarily put a halt to prostitution in England in the 1800s. However, when her son, the Prince of Wales, reached manhood, his shocking love affairs soon put the ladies back on the streets of London.

In America, the strict mores of its puritanical forefathers made prostitution difficult to accept. The first colonies frowned upon anything that was trivial or frivolous, including entertainment. Female actresses were not allowed to perform in the theater until the mid-1800s, and even then they were considered to be sinful. Prostitution existed in the United States, but it was kept underground. Eventually the more liberal states and territories either ignored it or learned to live with it.

With the Westward Movement and the opening of the American Frontier, prostitution began to flourish. Hundreds of thousands of young, healthy men left their homes and families behind in search of precious metals, land and adventure. Miners, farmers, shopkeepers, gun-slingers and gamblers pushed their way across the continent into a hostile land that fought their every step.

There were few women on the frontier. In 1849, the ratio was two women for every 100 men. It was a place where manhood was established by how tough a man was, how fast he could draw, and how much whiskey he could drink. To hold your liquor like a man was the highest compliment. It was a man's world where brawn and good health were more important than a college education.

These men lived in crude shelters, tents, and on occasion, a cave carved in the side of a mountain. They suffered from overwork, danger, fatigue, and most of all, the want of female companionship. Their daily lives lacked the warmth and comfort that only a woman could provide.

The first women to arrive were the ladies of easy virtue. They flocked to the frontier by foot, horseback and wagon — and they were not all glamorous. Most of the "ladies" wore simple clothing, however a few were clad in elaborate gowns. Some were in search of a husband, but the majority came for the same reason as the men—money and adventure!

These ladies elicited a great deal of excitement among the men. They moved into the available shacks and cabins and went to work at what they did best. The "fancy" ladies began providing a multitude of services that filled the needs of the young men as well as the older ones. They entertained, owned, or worked in the gaudy saloons, acted as dancing partners in the "hurdy-gurdy" houses and provided sexual favors, for a price.

The red light district in which the women lived became the social center of the community. Whiskey, prostitution and gambling blended together. Men came to town on payday to spend their hard earned money, and the women were eager to accept it.

These "fallen" women, however, supplied more than the pleasures of the flesh. Many were kind-hearted and provided companionship to the lonely men. Often a miner would be found sitting in the cabin of a "painted" lady while she mended his socks and sewed buttons on his shirt. When the men became ill or were injured, these ladies would nurse them back to health.

The mere presence of the gentler sex had a soothing effect upon the predominantly male society. One Montana miner said: "Many's the miner who'd never wash his face or comb his hair, if it wasn't for thinkin' of the sportin' girls he might meet in the saloons."[1]

A young man in California expressed his need for a women in a different way. After spending $150 for new clothing, which he couldn't afford, he traveled over 100 miles just to see a French woman who was dealing twenty-one. The sound of her voice was so exciting that he later wrote in his diary: "She's got a voice like music and just her speaking to me in that way put me all in a flutter."[2]

By the mid-1850s, "respectable" women were beginning to arrive in the frontier. They had traveled the prairies, endured hardships, and fought hostile Indians. These calico-clad females were eager to become part of the West. They fixed up the miserable shacks and planted flower gardens. Soon buildings and churches began to appear and the clergy followed close behind.

The "soiled doves" did not belong in the new morality that was spreading across the West. Since there could be no peaceful co-existence between the "good" women and the "bad" ladies within the communities, officers of the law began to impose fines upon the prostitutes. A few respectable women attempted to help these unfortunate ladies of easy virtue find redemption—but most of them were beyond that. The majority of the citizens didn't care what happened to them.

Since business was still flourishing, the ladies moved their shacks and brothels outside the city limits, putting themselves beyond the jurisdiction of the law. A few packed their trunks and headed for other, less moral towns, or moved back to the cities from whence they came. Most remained to live as social outcasts, working at the only profession they knew.

[1] **The Gentle Tamers**, by Dee Brown
[2] **The Diary of a Forty-Niner**, Edited by Chauncy L. Canfield

*"Let her many good qualities invoke leniency
in criticizing her failings."*

*Thompson and West,
History of Nevada County,
California, 1880*

CONTENTS

Cover Photo:
Courtesy of The Lake County Museum
Lakeport, California

Julie A. Knudsen, Graphic Artist

The "soiled doves" and red light districts were as much a part of the early West as the piles of mine tailings, canvas shacks and garish saloons that dotted the landscape. These ambitious ladies were caught up in the excitement of the frontier and the high demand for their professional services. Although their numbers were low in 1849, the ranks of prostitutes grew steadily as other American woman came West and newcomers arrived from nearly every country in the world.

Some of these colorful, if not socially acceptable, "ladies" were dressed in black silk stockings with scanty costumes, others in elaborate gowns with jewels. They brightened the drab frontier with their female chatter and drove the male population wild. Few if any, however, thought to look for the real woman who lay beneath the coldly-warm exterior and forced laughter.

Who was she, this seductive, often rowdy woman, who started her work as the sun's last rays began to disappear? Was she a captive who was caught in the web of poverty, a victim of circumstances, or a willing participant in her profession? Most likely, she was all of the above.

Many of these women came from other countries to escape poverty. They usually had no funds and the majority were uneducated and did not speak English. There were few ways in America for these women to survive. With luck they could marry, or work as a domestic — the alternative was to become a prostitute. Since prostitution paid better wages and the work seemed more exciting, most of the women chose the latter. They didn't have time to consider the consequences.

Most American women of the frontier became prostitutes because they were caught in a situation over which they had no control. Western employment, for the most part, belonged to the predominantly male work force. Regardless of their education, the majority of women were offered only the most menial and lowest paid work. For a young woman who was all alone, over-worked and desperate, prostitution was the logical solution. If she chose the menial job, she was still not respected by society. "Community's did not hesitate to use the needed services of these women, while simultaneously castigating them for their poverty."[1] So why wouldn't they turn to prostitution!

Several women enjoyed being a prostitute. It was their chosen way of life and they became willing participants in the world's oldest profession. These women were devoted to their work and enjoyed the material benefits and freedom they thought it offered. Unfortunately, their dreams of wealth seldom became reality—most ended up in the gutter, with a sick, abused body.

Almost all prostitutes had unsavory reputations. In the West, however, there were many kind, generous ladies of easy virtue. These women spread a silken web of good deeds that sparkled in the wilderness. They contributed to the local charities, hospitals and churches and were the first to lend a hand during a disaster, or offer assistance to the survivors.

During a flu epidemic in Saltese, Montana, a local madam had her "girls" go into the town and help take care of the ill. The girls were willing, and many lives were saved because of their tender care.

Mollie May, a madam of Leadville, Colorado, was known for her many kindnesses as well as her many indiscretions. When one of the local children was orphaned, she faced the outrage of the "proper" citizens and adopted the child. When Mollie died, she left enough funds to see that the child was cared for.

The soiled doves were good for the western economy and helped support the community. They spent their money locally, buying fancy clothing, expensive wines and ornamental jewelry. These women paid for business licenses, when required, and fines when they were arrested for breaking the law. The lawmen and ladies usually lived in harmony. There were seldom any special accommodations for women in the jails, so they learned to co-exist—it was easier on the taxpayer.

When historians recognize the businessmen of the early West, they often overlook the other entrepreneurs—wealthy madams like Josephine Hensley, Veronica Baldwin and Mattie Silks. These

[1] **Daughters of Joy, Sisters of Misery**, Anne M. Butler

women, and others like them, provided housing and employment for hundreds of women who otherwise would have been on the streets. They displayed a fine sense of business acumen, and played a significant role in the economy of the 19th century. In return, these ladies were ignored, refused admittance to the commercial clubs, and never accepted into society. They were even denied the protection of the law due to the nature of their business.

Although she was socially unacceptable, the western prostitute blended into the fabric of the frontier with an easy familiarity. This book brings to life the early West and the colorful ladies of ill repute who helped to tame an otherwise uncivilized land.

Due to the nature of this book, these stories have been carefully researched and documented through the generous assistance of historians, librarians and the special collection departments of several leading universities.

I have spent years reading old out-of-print books, biographies, newspapers dating from the 1800s to the mid-1900s, magazines, diaries, public records, and correspondence.

As with all history, especially that of prostitution, one must write with care and rely upon what others have written or recorded. In this book, I have attempted to create readable, accurate stories of these ladies of the night and provide an insight into their often sad, always touching lives.

— The Author

Timothy Gordon Collection, Missoula, Montana

◆───────────────────────────────◆

A lady of easy virtue

Chapter 1

SILK STOCKINGS AND
FANCY LINGERIE

T he heyday of prostitution, in America, occurred during the turbulent years of the early West when women were at a premium. It was an era of cowboys and Indians, gunslingers and fancy ladies. Elegant parlor houses and first-class brothels appeared in larger cities like San Francisco, Seattle and Denver. Shabby cribs and lower-class brothels sprang up in cowtowns and mining communities that were spread throughout the frontier. It was a time of adventure and danger, and a period in history when lonely men often called the red light districts their second home. "The mere mention of a bonnet on the streets of Denver in 1859 brought argonauts bolting to their doors, and a youth in another Colorado mining camp paid twenty dollars in gold dust for the initial pancake made by the region's first unmarried woman."[1]

Thousands of unattached females flocked to the womanless society in order to gain wealth and personal freedom. Most were inexperienced, illiterate and totally unprepared for the ways of the rugged West. The majority of these women were forced, out of necessity, to accept the only employment available, prostitution. As the members of this profession grew, a strict hierarchy was soon established. For the innocent, this was often a rude awakening, as they were at the bottom and caught in a situation from which there were few ways to escape.

At the top of the system were the courtesans or mistresses followed by lavish parlor houses and fancy brothels. The courtesan was usually a woman of beauty, intelligence and sophistication. She knew what she wanted and had the wit and charm to attain her goal. While the European ladies became the mistresses of royalty,

[1] **Beyond the Mississippi**, by Albert D. Richardson

the American women formed romantic attachments with gentlemen of power and great wealth. They were willing to provide a personal service in exchange for monetary gain and a successful career. The man's stature within the community forced society to accept his mistress and often guaranteed her respectability.

The parlor house was the next step in the hierarchy of prostitution. These establishments, which were often referred to as "boarding houses," always enjoyed a prime location. The decor was lavish and their luxury often surpassed the other homes in the neighborhood.

All parlor houses and high-class brothels had servants, a bouncer and the "professor." This gentleman supplied music for the ladies and guests during the evening hours. He played for a small wage, tips and drinks. The professor usually traveled the circuit visiting each house for a few weeks. Some were talented, others were not, but it wasn't the music the customer came to hear— he had other things on his mind.

The madam in these establishments was always sophisticated and discreet, and her "girls" were referred to as "boarders." There were about 20, elegantly clad, experienced prostitutes working in each house. The girls ranged from 18 to 30 years of age.

These ladies purchased their own clothing and wore the latest fashions in evening wear, afternoon costumes, and expensive lingerie, which was considered to be a business expense. "In San Francisco, as elsewhere, the parlor-house resident had to be not only beautiful but accomplished. A visit to a perfectly managed parlor house was much like a visit to a private home, and the prostitute resembled, in decorum and dress, the daughters of the house. Some writers wittily argued that the only difference, in fact, was that the prostitute was more attractive, more intelligent, and more accomplished than the young society lady."[1]

In order to ensure a profitable business, the madam had to attract quality customers through discreet advertising. One of the popular methods was to have her ladies dress in their finest and stroll leisurely along the promenade or ride in an open carriage through the park. On these excursions, a few of the women would carry their pet poodles. These soft, cuddly little dogs were a favorite

---

[1] **The Fair But Frail: Prostitution In San Francisco 1849-1900**,
  by Jacqueline Barnhart

of the parlor ladies, so no "decent" women dared to own one.

On occasion, the madam would send special engraved invitations to her opening soirees. These costly affairs allowed prospective customers the opportunity to meet her ladies. The guests were offered fine food, champagne and an evening of pleasure. The madam made up her losses by selling bottles of wine at 500 times their actual cost.

The most effective advertising, however, was a directory that could be found in the elite saloons, restaurants and hotels throughout the city. The first one appeared in New Orleans, and it was called *The Blue Book: A Gentlemen's Guide to New Orleans.* The book was very popular, but unfortunately not all the men were gentlemen.

These books contained names, addresses and descriptions of the parlor houses, or brothels, and the ladies who worked in them. The French and American women were at the top, with the French ladies noted for their experience in the boudoir. Many elite parlor houses also requested a letter of recommendation or business card from their customers before allowing them to enter the house.

The ladies were encouraged to charge their clothing, makeup and perfume to the madam's accounts. The credit of the madam was always excellent — unfortunately that of the girls' was worthless. The merchants usually added an extra 20 percent to the already high bills, and the ladies were constantly in debt to the madam. There was little, if any, money left for their future — these women lived only for the moment.

During their spare time, the parlor house ladies did fancy needlework, read books, or spent hours in the garden. They were served nourishing meals several times a day. Since their work was strenuous, the ladies ate steaks and roasts and drank large amounts of milk. It was a life of comfort and ease for that era.

In the evening, however, the parlor house prostitute paid her dues when she had to cater to a man's sexual needs. Once he entered her bedroom he usually forgot his breeding and background. The woman was considered fair game and required to do as he wished. She could never hurry the man she was entertaining. No matter how humiliating or painful it became, she had to pretend she was enjoying her job. Needless to say, a great deal of money was spent on the fancy sheets and pillowcases which were changed several times a night.

The parlor house clients were highly respected, prominent figures of the community and gentlemen of wealth. Upon arrival, the man was conducted to the parlor by the maid, and if he did not have a special woman in mind, the madam would select one for him. Following the introduction, they would converse a while before sitting down to a gourmet supper accompanied by expensive wines. Later, when he was ready to go upstairs, the maid would discretely collect the fee for the evening — there were no hints of commercialism.

The madam took care of any problems and assured the girls protection from the vice raids. There could be no disturbances from rowdy guests and the customer was guaranteed complete privacy. The madam always paid enough revenues and fees to the city, so the police left her house alone. She was also expected to make generous contributions to local charities and churches.

In return, the ladies gave the madam half of their fee, which was about $25, or more if the man spent the night. They also paid for their room and board and personal beverages. The girls were allowed to keep their own tips. Since parlor house prostitutes were not welcome at social gatherings, there was little to spend their money on. It was a restricted, lonely life that was only livened by the tinkle of a bell and the words, "company, ladies!"

The majority of the madams were prostitutes who were no longer attractive to men. They were experienced in the profession and ran the house with a firm hand. These women were also lonely and craved affection, but they seldom had a lover who cared about them. The girls were their companions. A few of the madams, like Denver's Mattie Silks and Laura Evans, chose to be madams because it meant upward mobility and the chance to become wealthy without catering to the personal needs of a man. None of the madams competed with the girls for a customer. These women rarely procured innocent victims or hired girls from the white slave trade — the parlor house prostitute could not be an amateur.

A lack of ventilation was characteristic of all parlor houses and brothels. The windows were seldom opened, and the houses reeked of stale smoke, stale drinks, and stale perfume. The tall, barred windows not only kept the fresh air out, they provided protection for the madam and her girls. The madam always had jewelry and money in her safe, and each lady had her own trunk filled with what valuables she possessed. Everything these women owned was kept in their one pathetic trunk. The barred windows also kept uninvited guests out. More than one man was known to climb over the rooftops to pay a visit to a fair lady, thus cheating the madam of her percentage.

As the Westward Movement continued to grow, towns like Bodie, Butte, Deadwood and Wallace sprang to life. Tales of rich gold and silver strikes, and instant millionaires, made headlines around the world. As the shortage of females on the frontier grew more pronounced, ruthless procurers began to recruit young European girls for shipment to America. In return, the girls were required to serve a term of years working for an employer — the employer, unfortunately, was usually a brothel owner.

Although many of these women were already prostitutes, others were often innocent victims who came to America to find a better life. They were uneducated, unskilled, and most did not understand English. A few managed to find husbands, some were indentured as domestics, but the majority were forced into prostitution. Since they had no choice, the women eventually learned to accept their fate. They blended into the womanless West, and were affectionately known by names like Irish Mary, English Rose and Dutch Em.

These multi-cultural soiled doves appeared throughout the frontier in both urban as well as the raw, untamed communities. They set up their businesses in canvas tents, flimsy shacks, and all available buildings. The women weren't elegant, but the men welcomed them with open arms. A touch of femininity had arrived, and the lonely males finally had a friendly place to hang their hats. As the West expanded, a few of the smaller structures were converted into brothels, which became the next step in the hierarchy of prostitution.

All of the houses of prostitution, whether they were in an urban area or the frontier, existed to cater to a man's needs. There was a world of difference, however, between an elite parlor house and a brothel, although both were often referred to as a "house."

Most brothels were situated in what was called the red light district or tenderloin. This was the designated area for the "houses of sin," saloons, and gambling establishments. The term "red light" is said to have originated in Dodge City, Kansas. Dodge City was a major stop for the railroad, and a convenient place for the train crews to visit the ladies of negotiable virtue. When these men entered the brothels, as they often did, they would leave their red lanterns outside so they could be located in case of an emergency. The madams soon realized that a red light was an excellent way to advertise, and the custom spread. The red light in front of a place of prostitution eventually became a law, and every brothel and crib had to display the light during the night. Many cities also insisted that a red shade or curtain be hung in the windows of these establishments during the day.

Pearl Starr, daughter of the petticoat bandit, Belle Starr, and a madam, took the law seriously. She placed a garish, star-shaped sign outside of her Fort Smith, Arkansas, brothel. The star was outlined in bright red, and it could be seen blocks away blazing its crimson welcome.

The term "tenderloin," originated in a district of New York City, where vice and police corruption were common. The area became notorious for its night life, crime and prostitution, and the name spread throughout the West.

The high-class brothels were located in a red light district and were a step down from the elegant parlor houses. They were not as well furnished and the madams were less discreet. The girls who worked in the brothels wore fancy, not elaborate clothing, and a considerable amount of makeup to conceal the dissipation that was a part of their profession.

These women ranged from 16 to 35 years in age. Age, however, was not always an important factor. Many times an older, experienced prostitute would earn more than a beautiful young girl. In her autobiography, Madeleine, a 19th century prostitute wrote: "Most women who have been ten years in the business are still under thirty and retain much of their youthful charm . . . but if they stay in the place where they are known, they become 'old-timers' to the men and do not receive the consideration shown the younger women."[1] It was important for the experienced prostitute to move from one location to another in order to appear youthful and maintain a successful career.

Although they were not elegantly furnished, the brothels still offered warm hospitality. They had comfortable saloons where the customer could enjoy an alcoholic drink and conversation with the prostitute before he requested her sexual favors. When he was ready, the man would ask the girl if she wanted to take a walk. She always said yes, but it is doubtful that the lady ever felt any romance or passion — sex was her business.

The girls in a brothel worked for less than the parlor house ladies, and they had a faster turnover. These women earned about $10 for their services. The price, however, could go higher depending upon the skill of the lady. No matter how much the prostitute earned, the madam always took her customary percentage. She also sold beer and whiskey to the customers at inflated prices — it was a profitable business.

Almost all brothels displayed a variety of signs and mottoes. One that was frequently seen was: "IF AT FIRST YOU DON'T SUCCEED, TRY, TRY AGAIN." In the larger houses a motto on the wall would often say: "LOTS OF BOARDERS — ALL THE COMFORTS OF HOME." The most popular sign, however was: "SATISFACTION GUARANTEED, OR MONEY REFUNDED." Unfortunately, the man seldom received a refund. He was usually presented with a wooden disk that was stamped, "GOOD FOR ONE."

A few of the madams would occasionally take their girls on what was referred to as a "summer vacation." They would set up large tents near, or within, a mining camp or town, and the ladies would go to work. The miners were delighted and it increased business. It also provided the girls with a change of scenery. When they returned to their brothels in the city, it was often with renewed energy. Madams like these were well liked by their girls.

Laura Evans was one of the popular madams. She was a lady

---

[1] **Madeleine, An Autobiography**, Persea Press, New York

from the South, who married at 17, had a daughter at 18, and deserted both her husband and daughter to become a prostitute. She worked in the houses of the West, where she was admired for her beauty, escapades, and a love of life that few women enjoyed.

Laura was one of the rare women who managed to save her money. In 1900 she opened a house in Salida, Colorado, and settled down to run a profitable business. Although Laura was a wild, boisterous women who rolled her own cigarettes and spouted profanity, she was adored by her girls as well as her customers. Laura was known for her generosity, kindness and loyalty to her employees. She ran a successful brothel until prostitution in Colorado became illegal.

While many madams were fair and kind, a few were known to be cruel and vicious. These few often had complete control over their girls who were usually so indebted to the madam that they couldn't leave. Although society seldom bothered to interfere in the red light districts, one madam finally went too far. The woman beat one of her girls so badly that the police were called to the scene. When the madam went to court, she was sentenced to jail for 80 days for inflicting "cruel torture upon one of her miserable women."

In comparison, Lou Harpel, a German madam, operated a first-class brothel on Mercury Street in Butte, Montana. Her girls were beautiful and in their early 20s. They enjoyed comfortable rooms, a good clientele and protection. Lou's relationship with her women was so close, that they referred to her as "mother." This was often the case in a brothel. The women were lonely and in need of love. A good madam would become a surrogate mother.

When the Civil War ended, many of the newly emancipated black women entered the profession. "Thrust into a society that did not want them, left with no means of support, some black women turned to prostitution in the West."[1] These women were used to slavery and merely traded one form of bondage for another. The more enterprising became madams who operated their own brothels, others worked in integrated houses and a few remained on their own. The black women were welcomed into the "sisterhood," and they blended easily into the rugged life of the early West.

All things considered, the courtesan and parlor house women

[1] **Daughters of Joy, Sisters of Misery**, Anne M. Butler

were better off than the average prostitute. A few managed to save enough money to open their own house, or start a small business. Some were lucky enough to marry. For most, however, it was just the first step down the long road of despair. As for the madam, she either retired wealthy, or remained in the business until the day she died.

Lola Montez, danseuse, actress, and one of the most sought-after courtesans of her era

THE NOTORIOUS LOLA MONTEZ

"Notorious I have always been, and never famous," were the words Lola Montez often used when describing herself. *Lola, the daughter of a Spanish beauty and a soldier in the British army, began her tumultuous life in Limerick, Ireland, in 1818. She rose from her humble origins to become a noted danseuse and one of the most sought-after courtesans of her era.*

Lola lived a life of confusion and make believe. She had the ability to invent whatever she pleased and the power to convince others it was fact. Although her dancing skills were not outstanding, she gained access to most of the royal courts of Europe. Lola was always seen in the company of gentlemen of wealth and position, and she was considered a fatal beauty.

King Ludwig of Bavaria was so smitten with her beauty, that he gave Lola a title and the keys to his country. She had an affair with His Imperial Majesty, Nicolas The First, of Russia. Her charms won the heart of Alexander Dumas, but she fell in love with his best friend, Alexander Dujarier, a French journalist.

When Lola came to San Francisco, the electrifying lady married Patrick Hull, the wealthy publisher of the San Francisco Whig. The couple moved to the small mining town of Grass Valley, California, where Lola found happiness for a brief period. Her home was lavish. She smoked Cuban cigars, ate imported foods and drank the finest liquor. It was said the eccentric lady bathed in champagne and dried herself with rose petals. She kept a pet bear and a live parrot who perched upon her shoulders.

Although Lola only spent two years in Grass Valley, she played an important role in the area's history, and she is well remembered. When Hull left the lovely dancer for his newspaper, she shook off her husband as easily as she had her other lovers and then moved on.

Lola's "Spider Dance" brought her a measure of success, but her bad temper, shocking antics, and outrageous love affairs eventually destroyed her life. On January 17, 1861, the notorious lady died alone, at the age of 42, in a squalid boarding house in the Hell's Kitchen District of New York City.

◆━━━━━━━━━━━━━━━━━━━━━◆

A moment of relaxation

Courtesy of the Denver Public Library, Western History Department
Marlin R. Parsons Collection, photo by Joseph Sturtevant

✦ ━━━━━━━━━━━━━━━━━━━ ✦

Belle Birdard's parlor house in Denver, Colorado

THE GIRLS THE MADAM AND THE PROFESSOR
STORYVILLE NEW ORLEANS - ABOUT 1910

Courtesy of the Amon Carter Museum, Fort Worth, Texas

◆ ───────────────────── ◆

"The Girls, The Madam, And The Professor"

Time for reflection

Mattie Silks at the age of 40

Chapter 2

IT HAPPENED ON
HOLLADAY STREET

◆━━━━━━━━━━━━━━━━━━━◆

Holladay Street in Denver, Colorado, was known as the wickedest thoroughfare in the West. Approximately one-thousand ladies of the evening plied their trade in the elegant parlor houses, fancy brothels and shabby cribs which lined both sides of the street.

Jennie Rogers, Rosa Lee, Lizzie Preston and Mattie Silks were among the many shady ladies who operated businesses in this infamous tenderloin. They were often referred to as the "giddy girls" of Holladay Street, and they were frequently arrested on charges of conducting lewd houses. At one time, things were so bad that the "girls" threatened to hire an attorney and carry their fight all the way to the Supreme Court.

Jennie Rogers was considered the most beautiful of the madams, but Mattie Silks was the undisputed Queen of Denver's Red Light District and the leading royalty for over two decades. She was a diminutive hell-raiser who drank expensive champagne, played the horses and enjoyed life to its fullest. Her "boarding houses" were known throughout the West for their beautiful young ladies and elegant decor.

Although Mattie was born on a small farm in Kansas in 1846, she was never a typical farmer's daughter. While the other girls dreamed of handsome husbands, Mattie had other plans. She knew at an early age that her chosen profession would be that of a glamorous madam in a high-class parlor house. When the opportunity arrived, Mattie, like most of the women who had crossed the Missouri before her, left her past behind.

In 1865, at the age of 19, Mattie Silks was running a parlor house in Springfield, Illinois. She was no doubt the youngest madam on the frontier and proudly claimed that she had never been a prostitute. It is believed that Mattie's early career was financed by a wealthy Kansas City madam.

As Mattie worked her way from Springfield to other boom towns, she operated only the finest houses and catered to the elite. The petite madam soon became known as the darling of the demimonde. It was said that Mattie resembled a vest-pocket edition of the famous Lillie Langtry, because of her clear, creamy complexion, impudent blue eyes and blonde curls piled high upon her head. She dressed in the latest fashions and all of her dresses were carefully tailored to conceal two special pockets, one for her gold coins and the other for her ivory-handled pistol. Life was tough in the West!

In 1876 Mattie brought her girls to Denver and opened a fashionable house on Holladay Street. Within a brief period, Mattie, who had always been a successful businesswoman, had what was considered a "carriage trade"; the money was rolling in! She had just about everything a reigning madam could desire, except a permanent lover. That wish, however, was fulfilled in 1877 when she met Cort Thomson, a cocky little foot-racer who wore pink tights and star-spangled blue running trunks.

Mattie's infatuation for the swaggering dandy was so great that she fought a duel with another Holladay Street madam over his affections. When the smoke from the women's blazing pistols cleared, the amorous Mattie found the other madam had wounded her man. He was not badly injured and soon a tempestuous love affair blossomed between Mattie and the flashy little runner who often bragged that he was too proud to do a day's work. The fact that Cort had a wife and daughter tucked away somewhere in his past didn't bother Mattie at all.

During the following years, he spent Mattie's money on gambling, expensive whiskey and eventually other women. At times he would ride his horse up the steps of her parlor house and through the door arrogantly demanding more money. On these occasions, Mattie would smile tolerantly and shower him with coins. Once Cort bought her a glittering cross covered with diamonds — but even that was purchased with Mattie's money. Nevertheless, she cherished his gift and only removed it when necessary.

Mattie's affair with the little dandy turned into marriage after Cort's wife died in 1884. At that time it was said that he only married Mattie for her money, not for her love. Two years later, when Cort was informed that his daughter had died leaving a small granddaughter, he refused to accept the responsibility of raising the unfortunate child. Mattie felt differently. She adopted the little girl and placed her in a good boarding home.

Cort died in 1900 when Mattie was 54 years old. She was still in love with the worthless man. In death, as in life, Mattie provided him with the best. His funeral was extravagant and her tears were many. It was estimated that during their relationship, Cort had borrowed or spent over $50,000 of Mattie's money.

Following Cort's death, Mattie began to show her age. She had grown plump over the years and her chin was no longer smooth and firm. Business, however, was still flourishing, so she hired "Handsome" Jack Ready, a large flamboyant man many years her junior. Ready, who was fond of money, became her bouncer and financial advisor. He soon became her lover. The couple lived a wild and extravagant life, and in 1923, when Mattie was 77, she finally married Ready. Mattie knew she was growing old and she wanted someone to provide comfort and care in her declining years.

They moved into a cottage on Laurence Street and Jack Ready remained true to Mattie until her death in 1929 at the age of 83. Her funeral was quiet; there were no songs or flowers. Mattie was buried beside Cort Thomson, who had always been her only love.

Prostitution in Denver had ended years before Mattie died, and her fortune had declined. Although it has been estimated that the petite madam had had almost two million dollars pass through her hands during her career, she left very little behind. Mattie's estate consisted of $4,000 dollars, a few pieces of jewelry and some property. All of it was divided between her adopted granddaughter and her husband.

Handsome Jack Ready did not get the fortune he had bargained for, and he died a pauper two years later. His burial expenses were paid for through a collection taken from the barrooms he frequented.

Courtesy of the Amon Carter Museum, Fort Worth Texas

Lil Lovell

During the heyday of prostitution, Holladay Street gained an unsavory reputation that spread across the West. The disgruntled heirs of Ben Holladay, for whom the street was named, petitioned the city fathers to change its name. They obligingly renamed it Market Street, but the sordid business conducted there went on as usual.

A few of the ladies who operated boarding houses after the name was changed were Annie Ryan, Bell Bernard, Lil Lovell and Veronica Baldwin, with the latter two arriving in the late 1890's. Both of these ladies occupied the same house on different occasions and their stories are unusual.

Lil Lovell was a tall, glamorous woman who had been a leading madam in Creede, Colorado. She moved to Denver and opened a fancy parlor house at 2020 Market Street. Within a short time, her business was so lucrative that she sent for her sister, Lois, to join her. Neither Lil nor Lois realized that their place of business would soon be one of tragedy.

Lois was also a beautiful woman, but much younger and less experienced than her sister, Lil. One evening, an important businessman visited Lois as a client and fell madly in love with the alluring prostitute. She returned his affections and he soon proposed marriage. Lois knew she could never marry her lover for it would destroy his career and ruin him socially. The respectable citizens of Denver did not openly associate with, or accept a woman who was a "soiled dove."

The man continued to plead with Lois and she realized the situation was hopeless. The next time he left town on a business trip, the young woman took a bottle of poison off of the shelf, swallowed its contents, and died within a few minutes. Lil discovered her sister's lifeless body the next day and blamed herself for inviting Lois to come to Denver. She buried her sister, but she could never bury the grief within her heart.

When the businessman returned, he was informed of his lover's suicide and immediately went to her grave. Standing alone in the cemetery, he looked down at the mound of earth that covered what once was a beautiful woman and realized that he did not want to live without her. He drew his pistol, put a bullet through his brain and fell beside the fresh grave of the woman who had loved her man too much to marry him.

Lil Lovell attempted to continue on with her own life, but things would never be the same as they were before. She missed Lois and the lonely days became endless. A few years later she, too, died, leaving an estate of over $40,000. All the money in the world could never make up the loss of her beloved sister.

Shortly after the death of Lil Lovell, the house at 2020 Market Street was occupied by Veronica Baldwin. She came to the infamous street as a notorious woman whose name had been splashed across the nation's headlines frequently from 1883 to 1887.

Veronica, a tall, slender, regal woman with magnetic hazel eyes, was the cousin of the multi-millionaire womanizer, E.J. "Lucky" Baldwin. Her name first blazed across the newspapers January 5, 1883, when she shot and wounded her famous cousin. At that time, she was employed by Baldwin as a teacher at his California ranch. The headlines in the *San Francisco Call* read:

A WOMAN'S REVENGE
Lucky Baldwin Shot by His Young Cousin, Veronica.

Yesterday at 10:00 o'clock a young woman who calls herself Veronica Baldwin, a cousin, shot E.J. Baldwin through the left arm at the level of the heart as he was leaving his private dining room on the second floor of the Baldwin Hotel. She fired at him from a distance of six feet, without warning. She was immediately disarmed and arrested.

Veronica admitted to the shooting, claiming that he first assaulted her, then he had her fired. She further said that she could have killed him, because she was a good shot — and that she wished she had killed him. Baldwin said his cousin had been blackmailing him and at the trial he declined to testify against her. Veronica left the state.

She appeared again in 1886, threatening to sue Baldwin for the support of a baby she claimed he had fathered. The threat was quietly handled. The next time Veronica made the headlines, it was to say that her cousin had had her committed to the state mental asylum at Napa, California. The next few years are not recorded.

Veronica reappeared in the late 1890s when she moved to Denver and opened a business on Market Street. It was said that Lucky Baldwin provided her with the money she needed. It was also said that the lady displayed no evidence of insanity!

The ordeal that she had been through, however, left its mark upon the unfortunate woman. Although Veronica was still young, lines were etched upon her comely face, her hair was prematurely gray, and she walked with a slow measured step. Miss Baldwin was no longer the same person that California newspapers once described as "the most beautiful girl on the Pacific Coast."

With Veronica, Market Street acquired a bit of class and dignity. Her parlor house was tastefully decorated with Victorian furniture and valuable paintings. She served fine French wine in crystal glasses, imported delicacies and, in season, fresh oysters brought in from the coast. All of Veronica's girls were beautiful and well-educated. They wore only the most stylish gowns and expensive perfumes. Disorderly conduct was never permitted and a gentleman who had consumed too much wine was discretely escorted to the door.

Her clientele were wealthy and famous and came by invitation. They were greeted at the door by a butler and led to the parlor where the distinguished madam awaited. Veronica always wore royal purple, decorated with a touch of white lace. She presented a regal figure and spoke with a gentle English accent. A visit to her parlor house was one that was not easily forgotten.

When Denver's Red Light District closed in 1915, Veronica calmly closed her business and moved into one of the most fashionable neighborhoods. She continued to live a quiet, dignified life. She never spoke of her past or of the baby she claimed Lucky Baldwin had fathered. It has been assumed that the child was taken from Veronica when she was placed in the asylum and raised by foster parents or its own father.

Although the lights of Denver's Red Light District have been dark for many years, Veronica Baldwin, Lil Lovell, and the darling of them all, Mattie Silks, will live on in history. They will be remembered, along with the other notorious ladies of Holladay Street, as a part of Denver's wild and colorful past.

SAVED FROM A LIFE OF VICE

Notorious Procuress Cheated of
Her Prey by a Demi-Mondaine

A pretty, blue eyed young woman arrived in the city last Tuesday night, intending to seek employment. At an employment office she met a woman who advised her to adopt a course of vice.

Before the recruit began her career she was saved, and last evening two city detectives escorted her to the Union depot and placed her on a train bound for the home of a relative.

At the police station the young woman was booked as Mary Anderson. That, however, is not her correct name. She came to Denver from a Wyoming town hoping to better her condition.

About 9 o'clock Tuesday night the woman, in company with a notorious procuress, rang the bell of a brothel, where she was referred to another. At the latter place arrangements were quickly completed. The strange girl was exceedingly pretty. She had large blue eyes, a great abundance of brown hair, her features were regular and her face as innocent as that of a little child. In less than half an hour the landlady was informed that the girl was innocent. Veronica Baldwin, the landlady, was quickly convinced the statement was only too true. A chance had come to warn an innocent beginner of the error of her ways, and Veronica, once the most notorious woman of the Pacific coast, the former mistress of "Lucky" Baldwin, was not slow to avail herself of it. She pleaded with the girl for the sake of mother and family to return to her home.

Miss Anderson was sent away from the house Tuesday night and placed in a respectable dwelling. Yesterday Captain Martyn was notified by Veronica Baldwin and detailed Detectives Burlew and McLeduff to investigate. The young woman was brought to police headquarters yesterday afternoon and placed in charge of the matron. Her story was believed by all who heard it and her gratitude was indeed touching. Last evening she was sent away to her relatives, the police department bearing the expense of transportation.

Rocky Mountain News, April 28, 1898

IN THE COURTS

KEEPERS OF BAGNIOS

Bell Bernard, Gussie Grant, Lizzie Preston, Jennie Caylor, Clara Dumont, Jennie Rogers, Bell Jewell, Eva Lewis, Mattie Silks, Emma Smith, Rosa Lee, Mary Smith, Anna Gray, Minnie Palmer and Clara Hayden, a lot of the "giddy girls" of Holladay Street, charged with keeping lewd houses, and who gave bond in the District court last week for their appearance in the Criminal court, were arraigned to-day before Judge Rodgers and pleaded "not guilty."

The girls have formed a pool to test this matter, and if they are convicted in the Criminal court, they will enter a plea to the jurisdiction by way of abatement and carry the cases to the Supreme court.

Denver Daily Times, September 4, 1886

Courtesy of the Colorado Historical Society

◆ ────────────────────────────── ◆

The House of Mirrors

The "House of Mirrors" was built in 1889 by Jennie Rogers, a popular madam of the late 1800s. It was an imposing structure that stood at 1942 Market Street in Denver, Colorado. If its walls could speak, they would no doubt tell of millionaires, blackmail, and greed. When Jennie passed away in 1902, most of the stories died with her. She did, however, leave a legacy of five bizarre faces, sculpted in rose stone, that for more than fifty years remained to peer down upon the once famous street.

The following paragraph, taken from the files of the Western History Department of the Denver Public Library, describes these strange figures:

At the top is that of a clear-eyed maiden on whose lips smiles joy. Below and to the left, framed in long hair, is a horribly sensual face, one eye closed in a leer above thick slobbering lips. Next is the stupid fat face of a glutton. Then comes the hard, cold face of a woman not much older than the young girl above. The fifth face, in the narrow ell of the house, and behind her, is that of an embittered old man with cruel eyes, his hairy mustache cushioned on bulbous jaws.

Although there have been many tales told about these strange faces, only Jennie Rogers knew their meaning. Did the presence of these faces represent a part of her colorful life, or were they put there as a bad joke that would live on after she was gone? Whatever the true story, Mattie Silks purchased the house shortly after Jennie's death and immediately placed a large M. SILKS upon the tile doorstep.

The House of Mirrors was the perfect setting for the dynamic Mattie. This opulent establishment had doorposts carved to represent phallic symbols, an elegant reception room and a parlor with plate-glass mirrors that covered the walls. The chandelier, made of hundreds of glass-faceted prisms, hung from an eight-foot mirrored ceiling and gave the room a shimmering beauty that reflected upon a golden harp and rich brocade chairs.

In the resplendent ballroom, Mattie's scantily-clad ladies entertained their wealthy customers. They drank expensive champagne and whirled around the parquet dance floor. These ladies would eventually lead the eager men up the stairs that were covered with Oriental carpeting, past the tall, slender windows and on into the fancy bedrooms. There were twenty bedrooms on the second floor. It was a house that suited the new owner, since both were bold and expensive, and the envy of Market Street. Mattie merrily presided over her mansion until the red lights of Denver were extinguished in 1915.

The next owner of the famous house was the Buddhist Church. Its members worshipped in the mirrored parlor and the soft-spoken priests taught a different kind of love; one of joy and a pure and peaceful life.

When the Buddhists left, the house became one of many warehouses that lined the street. The House of Mirrors fell into obscurity and disrepair. Eventually, like the rest of what had once been a part of Denver's Red Light District, it was dismantled and has become just another memory of a turbulent era.

Moral Conditions

FRENCH WOMEN RAIDED
Over One Hundred Pulled in from the Sinks and Dives

Over 100 French women were arrested yesterday afternoon on indictments from the Grand Jury.

From noon until nearly 5 o'clock, Main Street, West Denver, and Holladay from Seventeenth to Twenty-second, was a scene of great excitement. Sheriff Wilbur sent Sheriff Wheeler with about 30 assistants to make the raid. The officers had two omnibusses drawn by six white horses each. As fast as a load was obtained it was sent to the Court House and the omnibusses returned for more . . . Holladay and some of the cross streets in this vicinity, has not witnessed such a scene in many a day . . . Many of the inmates had not arisen from their drunken slumbers and debauchery of the night before. Some swore, some cried and others laughed. Frail women in frailer garments were hurrying from room to room. Escape was impossible. They were herded like sheep. Some of the late raisers (sic) had to be given time to dress. One woman hastily placed a placard "for rent" on her door and hid in a trunk . . . Holladay Street was thronged.

Chatter, Chatter, Chatter

And these women! Their talk was like the confusion of the Tower of Babel. Some were mad, some were sullen, some laughed, some danced, they all wanted beer and cigarettes.

Old and Young
Some were young—in their teens. The hair of others was growing gray and their faces hardened in sin . . .

Some Had Cots
There were only a few cots and they were given to those who were sick. One of the girls known as "Big Em" was given a cot. She weighed three-hundred and ten pounds, and in climbing the steps had to stop and lean on the banister to rest. Those who had cots went to bed semi-dressed. Hats, wraps and dresses were hung up on nails in the rooms. Here and there were hung handsome undergarments as fine as the dry-goods house of the city can afford.

Thoughts for the Sick Girl
They are thoughtful of each other. "Where is Little Annie?" "She is sick and can hardly sit up" said one of the girls in a pleading voice to the deputy sheriff. The inmates of the room looked it over and saw that every cot was taken. "I will give Annie my cot" said one. "She can have mine" said another. Everyone who had a cot offered it to the sick "Little Annie" as they called her.
Excerpted from: The Denver Republic
Saturday, May 4, 1889, p.6

◆━━━━━━━━━━━━━━━━━━━━◆

"Squirrel Tooth" Alice

*This Dodge City prostitute has the haunting beauty
of the cow town era.*

Chapter 3

WORKING GIRLS

T he red light districts gave little evidence of the "romance" of the early West. Within those desolate streets, where prostitution flourished, there was no silken veil to hide the ugliness of raw, naked vice.

Prostitution existed in urban communities, mining camps, logging centers, cow towns and near the army posts. In these areas the population was overwhelmingly male. The demand for female contact, of an intimate type, was so great that the local men carefully guarded their wives and daughters — so the fancy ladies took over.

When a soiled dove lost her youthfulness and charms, she started down the steps of prostitution and left the comfort and protection of the parlor house and high-class brothel behind. Many times she also traded the busier urban areas for the more rural communities and frontier towns of the West.

If the woman remained in the city, she usually joined the other ladies who worked in the volume brothels and saloons, or became one of the dance hall or hurdy-girls. She was still, however, considered to be above the level of the crib prostitute.

The volume brothel catered to a brisk trade and offered no amenities. The furniture was dilapidated, carpets worn, and the shabby bedrooms opened off the hallway into the street — it was set up for business. The woman was required to sit in a tiny cubicle and entice her customers. She usually wore a low-necked, knee-length dress and black silk stockings. It was her job to openly solicit the men who sauntered the sidewalks inspecting the wares of the various women. Her words were often: "Come in, dearie." It was a degrading experience, especially for the ex-parlor house lady.

The girls employed in these brothels worked in shifts. They were older, less attractive, and most used drugs or alcohol — it was one way of survival. The madams offered quantity, not quality, and they wanted a quick turnover with a fast profit. The men came to a brothel for one reason, and they were in a hurry to get on with it. It was a house without rules and anything the man wanted he received — even if it was degrading to the woman. A fast prostitute could take care of as many as 25 men, or more, during her very busy shift.

Unlike the parlor house, where the linen was changed after each visit, the volume brothel seldom bothered to change the sheets at all. It was the type of place where a girl preferred being busy, as it made her time go faster.

Since these prostitutes were not respected members of society, they were considered "public" people. The newspapers enjoyed publishing, and enhancing, their often sordid stories. These articles provided the local men with a hearty laugh and gave the "proper" woman an opportunity to gather her cloak of respectability around her, secure in her own safe environment.

On January 24, 1891, *The Denver Times* carried the following news item:

WHERE IS DIRTY ALICE?
Please Address All Information to Deputy Sheriff James Wilson

Deputy Sheriff James Wilson is very anxious to find Minnie Smith, who is also known as "Dirty Alice." Alice is the woman who was recently fined by Justice Palmer for being intoxicated. She promised to bring the money to pay her fine to the court room if she was allowed to go home, and as none of the officers cared to be her escort she was allowed to go. She failed to return, however, and now Mr. Wilson has been deputized to find her, and put her in jail. He is not very joyful over the task.

There was no escape for these women. If Minnie Smith, or Alice, had been attempting to change her profession for a better life, the newspaper story most likely would have destroyed any chance she might have had. One such woman tried over and over to leave her unsavory profession. She had learned to be a seamstress and was successfully employed at that trade during her off hours. Due to continuous newspaper harassment, she finally gave up and left the area, only to continue on as a prostitute.

While most of the prostitutes hid their hatred and distaste behind lavish smiles, some of them enjoyed their jobs. They were nymphomaniacs who were so devoted to their profession that they spent their vacations working in other brothels. Many traveled from location to location with guaranteed bookings. A few were so popular with the men that the madams advertised their appearances in advance so the girls would have a full schedule when they arrived. These prostitutes seldom left their rooms, except to eat.

In the larger cities, many of the volume brothels hired their prostitutes by the week. These women were a cut above the norm and each had been examined by a doctor before seeking employment. They worked for a pimp, who would first take them to the brothel so that the madam could pick who she wanted for the coming week. When he returned with the women they immediately went to work. Their earnings were kept for their pimp, who collected both the money and his girls at the end of the week. The women were not allowed to leave the brothel during that week and the pimp gave them only a small amount of what they had earned — he kept the rest for himself.

In return, the pimp took care of their medical expenses, fines, and bailed them out of jail, when necessary. Once in a while he even provided a little love. The love, however, was given only if the woman had had a good week — she usually tried very hard to please her pimp, as his "love" was all she had. If she became pregnant, the woman was on her own; no pimp wanted a woman who couldn't work.

Needless to say, the pimp was a very unpopular man who was despised by almost everyone, especially other men. He preyed on lonely, desperate women and managed to establish an emotional bond with them. These women were already unstable and insecure, and often, he was the one who had led them into prostitution in the first place. Once they were established in the profession, he sat back and lived off of their earnings. Even the small amount of money the woman received meant little to her. She usually spent it on cheap perfume and lingerie, as her needs were few.

Although the pimp and the madam both sold flesh and exploited the women — it should be remembered that it was the pimp who seduced the girl into prostitution, alcohol and drugs, not the madam.

The soiled doves in the more rural communities generally enjoyed a measure of respect and greater freedom than the women in the cities. The brothels were smaller, with anywhere from two to seven girls. Its furnishings were shabby, but clean, with battered chairs, worn linoleum and old calendars for wall decorations. These houses did a good business, especially when the rowdy men came roaring into town with their pockets filled with silver dollars. They were whiskey-thirsty, and women-hungry, and ready to spend their money.

The customers of the frontier prostitute were mostly laborers, miners, cowboys and gun-slingers. She seldom made the money she could have earned in the city and it is doubtful that any of her customers were gentlemen of wealth. However, she had a better chance for marriage in the cow towns where people were more tolerant of others.

The men usually called the prostitute by her name. To them she was a person, not just another female body. More than one of the soiled doves have been known to trade their fancy finery for a calico housedress and a successful marriage. Historians carefully guard these ladies' names from outsiders, as their descendants are often the leading citizens of today.

All of the madams in both urban or rural areas, had two things in common. They were constantly on guard for signs of suicide and drunkenness. When the girls became depressed they would frequently take an overdose of laudanum (a form of opium). The madams also had to ensure that a woman did not drink to excess — the customers didn't want an unattractive, drunken prostitute who could not handle her job.

———————◆———————

No western city or town was complete without its saloons,

gambling establishments and dance halls or hurdy-gurdy houses. The hurdy-gurdy was a form of hand organ with strings, keys, and wooden wheels that produced music when the handle was turned. It was first used in Europe and became a popular musical instrument in America during the 1800s. The majority of the dance halls used these machines for music, and they were called "hurdy-gurdy houses." The ladies who worked as dancing partners in a hurdy-gurdy house were called hurdy-girls or hurdies.

The saloons and hurdy-gurdy houses were located throughout the Western Frontier. They were usually long, narrow frame buildings with a bar on one side and dance floor on the other. A hallway with several small rooms was in the rear. These rooms were rented to the customer who wanted more than a dance, and to the hurdy-girls who chose to entertain a man after, or during, working hours. Not all of these girls were prostitutes; most earned a good salary from dancing and serving drinks. The dance was often free, but the man knew he had to buy both himself and his partner a $1 drink after each dance. The girl usually drank cold tea — she didn't want to become intoxicated and lose her ability to follow her partners. A popular hurdy could take the floor with 50 men or more during the evening, which meant she earned at least $50, half of which she gave to her employer. It was a good wage for that era and unless the girl was greedy, she had no need to use a room. A few of the hurdy-girls worked part time to supplement their family's income. Others, however, did rent the rooms and entertain customers. The majority of the hurdy-girls received more respect than the average prostitute.

One of the favorite dance-hall girls and entertainers in Dodge City, was the beautiful Dora Hand. Dora was an opera star from Boston whose career was marred by tuberculosis. She came to the West hoping the dry air would heal her lungs. Dora entertained the cowboys nightly in the Grey Lady Saloon, where her clear bell-like voice cheered the hearts of all the customers, especially the Mayor, James (Dog) Kelley. The two soon became close friends.

Dora not only had a lovely voice, she was also known as an angel of mercy. When her night at the Grey Lady ended, Dora would change into a simple calico dress and become the "Lady

Bountiful of Dodge City." She was never too busy to visit a sick child or feed a hungry family. On Sundays Dora would lead the members of the congregation in their hymns. She was so loved by the citizens that the respectable women often complained that Dora was interfering with their "duties" and deeds of mercy.

One evening, Jim Kelley became ill and had to have surgery. In his absence, Dora and another entertainer moved into Kelley's cabin. A few nights later, two shots rang out and the lovely soprano was dead. A man who had a grudge against Kelley had tried to kill him, but instead had accidentally murdered the beloved Dora Hand.

When Sheriff Bat Masterson, and assistant City Marshal, Wyatt Earp, caught the murderer, he was astonished to find that he had killed a lovely lady and not his enemy, Kelley. Dora was given the largest funeral the city had ever witnessed, and the legend of the dance-hall singer, who may not have been a pure angel, grows stronger with each passing year.[1]

◆

"The social gulf between the first class courtesan and those who have become dregs of prostitution is as great as the gulf between the sheltered woman in her home and the streetwalker."[2]

The next step down the ladder of destruction was that of the crib prostitute. Most, but not all, of these fallen women worked for a pimp, and many followed the boom-towns of the West. The women in camps or mining towns would set up their business in a row of tents which could easily be taken down when they moved. In the larger cities they operated out of a hovel referred to as a "crib."

The crib was one of a string of small frame buildings located in the most disreputable section of the red light district or in an area referred to as the "row" or the "alley." These miserable dwellings were wide enough for a door and two small windows. There was a parlor in front, a bedroom in the rear, and a common privy in the back. They were devoid of any comfort and rented for anywhere from $8 to $20 a week in advance.

These structures were scantily furnished. The bedroom was just large enough for an iron bed, wash stand, kerosene stove and the woman's small trunk. It always smelled of lysol or carbolic acid.

[1] **Wyatt Earp: Frontier Marshal,** by Stuart Luke; **The Barbary Coast,** by Herbert Asbury
[2] **Madeleine, An Autobiography,** Persea Press, New York

"The bed itself was dirty and usually rickety and dilapidated. It was covered by coarse sheets and a bright colored spread, and across the foot of the bed was thrown a piece of red or brown oilcloth. This was to protect the spread's being soiled by the boots or shoes of the customers."[1]

Although the men never removed their shoes, they always took off their hats when visiting the lady. No self-respecting prostitute would do business with a customer unless he removed his hat in her presence.

Most of the women made a pathetic attempt to give their crib a personal warmth. Each cherished her few possessions and tried to make her dwelling different from the others. There would often be a few pictures of her family or her pimp, and needlepoint mottoes reflecting upon the virtues of motherhood and morality. She always had her name carved above the door to let the men know who she was or perhaps to just let people know she existed.

Women who worked in a crib did not sell romance, the man was not allowed to remain unless he paid for the privilege. On payday all the cribs played to standing room only and the men complained if the girl spent too much time removing her clothing. On these days the majority of the women wore very little attire. From dusk to dawn they labored in their "workshops" as the pimps would have the men lined up with their money in one hand and their hat in the other. A fast prostitute could accommodate as many as 80 men a night — they were in and out in a matter of minutes.

By this time, the woman was usually desperate. She had sunk to the level where she had no protection and lived a life of social rejection. A fallen woman could never accuse a man of rape, as she had given up that right. In her autobiography, Madeleine tells of a visit to the row in Butte, Montana: "Despite my shuddering horror, the sight fascinated even while it repelled me . . . I was sickened and faint at the horror of it . . . I drew my skirts back from contact with the poor creatures who represented the seamy side of prostitution."[2]

Not all the women who worked alone lived in a crib or had a pimp. Some were fortunate enough to make sufficient money to live in their own house or cottage. Julia Bulette was one of these

[1] **The Barbary Coast**, by Herbert Asbury
[2] **Madeleine, An Autobiography**, Persea Press, New York

women. She kept a fancy cottage on the row in Virginia City, Nevada, and she became a legend.

Julia had traveled through many western towns before she arrived in Virginia City in 1863. Her cottage was located in a prime spot at the end of the row of cribs on the corners of North and D Streets. It had lace curtains at the windows, a Brussels carpet and comfortable furniture. Her bedroom was elaborate, for Julia was a popular prostitute who usually chose her own customers and was reputed to receive as much as $1,000 a night for her favors.

She was kind and well liked by the miners; her generosity and donations to charity earned a measure of respect and gratitude. Julia nursed the sick and injured men back to health, fought a smallpox epidemic, fed the poor, and because of her help to the fire department, she became an honorary member of the Virginia City Company Number One.

In 1867, at the age of 35, Julia Bulette was murdered. She was found strangled, shot, suffocated and severely beaten — all of her personal possessions were stolen. The male population was shocked while the respectable women felt that she got what she deserved. Her friends gave Julia the most expensive funeral the city had ever seen and all the saloons closed for the first time in their history. Julia was allowed a Catholic service, but she could not be buried in consecrated soil, due to her profession. Her lonely grave lies about a mile east of the city. Although the plain wooden marker merely says "JULIA," her good deeds and kindnesses have become a part of the many legends of Virginia City's colorful past.

————◆————

All prostitutes feared an unwanted pregnancy as much as they feared a social disease. When a woman found she had a disease, she could have it treated and return to work in a few weeks. When she became pregnant it meant a loss of work and the responsibility of raising a child.

Prostitutes could not practice the common forms of birth control — abstinence or withdrawal, as their livelihood depended upon an active sex life. European women used a form of intrauterine device made from beeswax which formed a cervical cap or pessary. American women did not have access to these devices.

Few knew of their existence and most could not have afforded them if they had known about them.

The majority of the soiled doves ended up with an abortionist, who usually did a bad job and left them sterile, or they attempted to abort the child themselves, which often destroyed their reproductive systems. It was also discovered that "regular use of opiates caused disruption or total cessation of menstruation and it was possible that prostitutes used opiates as form of birth control."[1]

If a wealthy prostitute did have a child, she would usually place it with a good family and pay for its care. The poorer woman had few choices. She could let a relative adopt it, or put it in an orphanage. The other alternative was to attempt to raise the child herself. This, however, was an unfortunate arrangement, as the woman could barely take care of her own needs.

———————◆———————

At the bottom of the profession there was the streetwalker, a woman who lived in a grey world of disease, alcohol and drugs. Her beauty had been replaced with lines of dissipation and age, and there was no place for her to go. Not even a pimp would have taken her. She walked the streets desperately looking for a customer and would take any price, even a drink in exchange for her favors.

This woman, who was once sought after, now had to stand alone in dark, shadowy doorways so the man would not be able to see what she looked like — there was no more hope — the next step could be only one thing, suicide.

From the parlor house at the top of the profession, to the moral and physical decay of the streetwalker, the western prostitute always walked a lonely path. Although these women were considered immoral, it must be remembered that it was acceptable for a man to visit a prostitute, but the woman was condemned for being one.

---

[1] **Opiate Addiction in America, a Dissertation**, Rice University, 1979, P. 93, by David Courtright.

SUICIDE BY POISON

A FALLEN WOMAN ENDS HER
DAY WITH MORPHINE

*A Tumble-Down Row in West Denver
the Scene of Squalor and Death*

West Holladay Street was this afternoon the scene of a suicide which threw the inhabitants of that part of the city into a frenzy of excitement and caused nearly all the women in the neighborhood to emerge from the humble tenements which line the greater thoroughfare, and stand, bareheaded, with arms akimbo about the waist.

*BETWEEN TWELFTH AND THIRTEENTH
STREETS STANDS A LONG ROW*

of two-story, very rickety frame tenements, which at one period in a very long lifetime have had a coat of limewash smeared over them. The place is inhabited by people, many of them of the lowest stripe, several of the apartments, or more properly speaking dens, of the structure being occupied by

FALLEN WOMEN

and low lived males who consort with them. Chinese laundry shops with bright colored posters covering the window panes, on the first floor here and there lend a little relief to the eye and serve to break up the monotony of the repulsive view. About fifty steps from the north corner of the room is a flight of narrow, very dangerous steps, leading to the upper story, and further down, another flight.

Today at two o'clock a policeman paced up and down in front of the first entrance, his every move being watched by a curious crowd of hangers-about who heard that one of

THE WRETCHED INMATES

had committed suicide. The coroner had been called for and soon arrived, and proceeded up stairs.

There, in a small room, black with smoke of ages and the air which was overpoweringly unpleasant, lay stretched on a dirty bed, a woman, dead. Her name was Mrs. Wringer.

The story was she had been drinking heavily, her "husband" a Frenchman and "Sheeney," had deserted her, and last night

SHE SWALLOWED

a big dose of morphine. On the bed beside the dead woman, lay a terrier, her pet, whining piteously.

The remains were taken away for inquest and the dog followed the undertaker's wagon.

The Denver Times, December 15, 1886

◆ ━━━━━━━━━━━━━━━━━━━━━━━━━ ◆

*Julia Bulette, Virginia City, Nevada's
legendary prostitute with a heart of gold*

THE HANGING OF JOHN MILLIAN

On January 20, 1867, the legendary Julia Bulette's dead body was found in her home. She was lying on her left side with her feet halfway out of the bed. Sometime during the night she had been strangled, shot, suffocated and severely beaten. The press called her murder atrocious and wrote that it was "outrageous and cruel."

Several months after Julia's funeral, the law arrested John Millian, a French drifter, who claimed he had not murdered her, but said he knew it was going to happen. Due to the town's hatred for Millian, a jury was very difficult to select. The officials couldn't find 12 men who were unbiased, and women in 1868 were not allowed to vote. A jury, however, was eventually chosen and the accused man was found guilty. He was condemned to die by hanging.

At dawn, on April 27, 1868, John Millian met his fate. The hanging became a spectator event, with everyone hoping to catch a glimpse of the murderer. Excited people came by stage, horseback, or on foot from the nearby towns. All of the saloons were closed for the second time in the history of Virginia City, the first being the day of Julia's funeral.

Forty deputies and the National Guard, in full uniform, escorted the carriage carrying Millian and Father Manogue, priest of St. Mary's Catholic Church. The physician's vehicle followed the prisoner, and behind it came the news media and a coffin draped in black accompanied by the undertaker and his assistants.

The gallows were already in place and several thousand people gathered. The prisoner spoke a few words in French, contending he didn't understand English well enough to defend himself. He kissed the priest, mounted the scaffold, and within two minutes Millian was declared dead.

The murder of Julia Bulette was avenged, and the crowd returned to Virginia City to open the saloons and celebrate. Throughout the entire event, Julia was never referred to as a woman of easy virtue. It was obvious the people finally accepted the goodness in her, despite her profession.

From Women of the Sierra, by Anne Seagraves

Courtesy of Special Collections Division, University of Washington Libraries
Photo: Eric A. Hegg #2442

Ladies of the line in Dawson, Yukon Territory

◆————————————————————◆

A brothel in Saltese, Montana

Although this "house" is far from elegant, it is typical of all the brothels of the Western frontier.

Courtesy of History & Industry, Seattle, Washington, Pemco Western Collection

A group of "working girls" in an early mining camp

A *"Hurdy-Gurdy" dancer in Helena, Montana*

*A 1905 mug shot of a prostitute
in Bonner County, Idaho*

SHERIFF'S OFFICE BONNER COUNTY

No.................

Name....Eugiene Flaurent....

Alias......."Nina"...."........"

Residence.....................

Nativity....French............

Occupation....Common Prostitute

Criminal Occupation............

Age..30...Height.5-5 1/2.....Weight.150...

Build....Heavy....Complexion..DK....

Eyes..Brown....Hair..Black....

Mustache.........Beard.........

Arrested..Aug 1st 1905.........

By....RW Augertine...........

Crime....Disturbance.........

Disposition....$10.00.........

Scars, etc...3 inch Scar........
Under lower lip

Courtesy of Douglas McDonald, Grantsdale, Montana

✦ ─────────────── ✦

Bonner County "rap sheet"

Courtesy of Bodie State Historic Park, Bodie, California
Photo: © Jill A. Lachman

Lottie Johl

Chapter 4

THE LOVE STORY OF
LOTTIE JOHL

♦⎯⎯⎯⎯⎯⎯⎯⎯♦

I n 1879 a little girl cried, "Good-bye, God! We're going to Bodie," an apt description for one of the West's wildest and richest mining towns.

Bodie, California, 8,200 feet above sea level, was a place where men of the 1800s dreamed of wealth and few were blessed. It was a town noted for violence and death, where whiskey arrived 100 barrels at a time and the term, "Fire in the hole," meant drinks for the house.

Bodie's Main Street was one mile long with frame buildings on either side; every other one was a bar or gambling parlor. Death was common, for at least one man was shot to death daily. Miners worked for $24 a week and everyone lived for the moment. It was to this town that Lottie came to pursue her profession, and it was in this town that Lottie died.

The known history of Lottie began in Bodie in about 1882. Lottie, like most of the women in her profession, attempted to keep her past a secret. In her case, however, a few exciting facts have been recently uncovered.

In 1992, a woman visiting the museum at Bodie State Park, saw Lottie's portrait hanging on one of the walls, and calmly announced the woman in that portrait was her great-great-grandmother. It was from this woman, Lottie's great-great-granddaughter, that a part of the early portion of Lottie's life has been uncovered.

Lottie was born on a farm in Iowa in 1855; there is no record of her parents. We do not know if the farm was large or small, but we can assume Lottie's life was not easy and that she received very little education. A farmer's daughter of that era worked from dawn until dusk, with little reward.

Although eligible young men were usually rare in rural Iowa, Lottie managed to find herself a husband. *She was an attractive, lovable girl, with soft hazel eyes, and light curly hair, and a mouth curled up in the corners that seemed to be smiling all the time.*[1] Lottie was noted for her merry laughter and gentle disposition.

During this marriage a little girl was born. Something went wrong, however, for Lottie divorced her husband and took her daughter away. She unsuccessfully attempted to support herself and the child, but Lottie was not skilled in any trade. To make matters worse, a divorced woman in the 1800s, was not considered to be respectable.

After many months of struggle, Lottie either left her daughter with her parents or her ex-husband, and moved away from Iowa. Because she was a gentle girl, it must have been a rough life, with few opportunities. It is not known how, or when, she became a prostitute. Perhaps she started as a hurdy-gurdy dancer and eventually drifted into the profession.

Since Lottie was a farm girl, she no doubt worked the more familiar rural towns before heading for the larger cities. Without a surname or sobriquet, it is almost impossible to trace her travels through the West. There were many girls named Lottie.

It can be assumed that Lottie was a high-class prostitute who worked only the better "houses." She appeared to be a woman of class and distinction with a strong sense of decency, despite her profession. With all these attributes, why did Lottie come to the rough town of Bodie? — Perhaps it was to meet her fate.

On a warm summer's day in 1882, at the age of 27, Lottie stepped down from the stage and calmly looked around the town. The lone woman passenger thanked the driver for a safe trip over the rough road into Bodie, then she asked directions to "Virgin Alley" or "Maiden Lane." The driver, along with the locals who met the daily stage, appeared shocked at the young woman's request. Both Virgin Alley and Maiden Lane were really one street and a part of the red light district. This pretty little thing certainly didn't look like she belonged there. The men shook their heads in dismay, and one politely offered to show her the way.

Bodie's red light district adjoined the twisted alleys of

---

[1] **The Story of Bodie**, by Ella M. Cain

Chinatown. It was an area of cribs, brothels and often a place of desperation. Along these grim streets and alleys, women of all ages and with varying degrees of beauty, offered "love" for a price. The red light ladies seldom ventured uptown during the day, as they were not welcome. When the sun's last rays disappeared, they dressed in all their finery and frequented the numerous saloons and dance halls that lined Main Street. A fancy lady would whirl around the floor with an eager partner, then they would disappear into the darkness from whence she came.

There were two high-class brothels in Bodie: The Highgrade and The Ozark. The women who worked there had names like Rosa May, "Peek-a-boo," and "Beautiful Doll," and, they all appeared to be ladies of quality. Although it was apparent that Lottie worked in one of these houses, she was a step apart from the other girls, for Lottie was special — she cared.

Lottie settled easily into the life of the rough mining town. She spent her days visiting with the other girls, and in the evening she joined in the excitement and bright lights of Main Street. Lottie loved to dance and she soon became one of the most sought-after partners. Her lively dancing attracted the men and her friendliness put them at ease. One night while Lottie was dancing with an admirer, she noticed a large man watching her every movement. His name was Eli Johl, a man who had fallen for a woman he considered to be the prettiest in Bodie — Lottie!

Johl was a rough, simple man, not known for his social climbing. He was a German immigrant who was co-owner of one of the two butcher shops in Bodie. The other partner was Charles Donnelly, a man whose wife was a haughty woman of English decent. While Donnelly stood behind the counter in a white apron and waited on the customers, Johl did the dirty work, slaughtering and packing the meat. In the evening he would drift down to Main Street for a little diversion. It was there he saw Lottie and lost his heart.

Within a short time Johl began showering the pretty lady with jewelry, money and attention. Although he knew she was a prostitute, her love was more important to him than her past. Lottie had always been used and never loved; for her it was a new experience.

She eventually returned Johl's affection and they were legally married. The "proper" women of Bodie were aghast, more than a few men were envious, and Mrs. Donnelly, the wife of Johl's partner, was furious. She felt the marriage was a direct insult to her own social standing and attempted to end the partnership between Eli Johl and her husband. The partnership, however, was stronger than Mrs. Donnelly for it was business as usual for the two men.

Eli bought his wife a five-room cottage on Main Street, near the butcher shop. He filled it with the finest furnishings money could buy, for he wanted his wife to have only the best. Lottie was proud of her home and her husband. She and Eli were so in love they decided to have a party to share their happiness. Eli sent carefully selected invitations to his friends and Lottie cooked all kinds of fancy food; she was sure it would be a successful event. When Mrs. Donnelly found out, she discouraged everyone from attending, claiming a prostitute did not deserve such a fine life. No one came to Lottie's party and Eli knew she would never be accepted. He didn't care about himself, but he knew his wife's heart had been broken.

Eli and Lottie grew close, wrapping themselves up in their love for each other. Lottie was a good wife. Although she must have missed the friendship of other women, and dancing, she never complained to Eli. When he arrived home from the butcher shop each evening, he was greeted by a warm hug and supper on the table. Perhaps he, too, missed the excitement of his former life — if he did he kept it to himself.

Mrs. Donnelly was considered to be the local artist and cultural expert. She spent long hours working at her easel creating paintings which were sold to the local citizens. Her paintings weren't very good, but the people of Bodie thought they were wonderful. While Mrs. Donnelly painted, Lottie sat at her living room window and watched the people passing by.

As Eli saw his wife grow lonelier, he decided she needed a hobby. If Mrs. Donnelly could paint, he felt his Lottie could probably do it better. Eli purchased an easel, yards of canvas, paints and expensive frames, and Lottie became an artist. Her first attempts were awkward, but she did have a certain flair. Lottie's pictures soon covered the walls of their home. Eli was proud and wanted to share his wife's accomplishments. Lottie's past, unfortunately, continued to follow her. She was shunned by all, there was only Eli to admire her art. Today, however, others can enjoy Lottie's paintings, as one of her mountain scenes, in its elaborate frame, hangs in the museum at Bodie.

When the local citizens started planning an extravagant masquerade ball at the Miner's Union Hall, Eli saw this as an opportunity to show the people of Bodie how much Lottie had changed. He sent to San Francisco for the finest costume money could buy. Eli thought the town might accept his wife if they would only take the time to know her. The ball was to be her own coming-out party.

When the night of the ball arrived, Eli remained home so that no one would recognize Lottie. She went to the event alone dressed in her exquisite attire. *The dress was a white satin, all covered with seed pearls and diamonds (just imitations, of course), but a sparkling like the real thing. On her blonde curls were set a crown made of the same kind of diamonds and pearls.*[1] Lottie was beautiful. Nothing as fine as her costume had ever been seen by the citizens of Bodie, and she was shining with happiness. No one suspected it was Mrs. Johl, for a woman with her background would never have dared to attend an event like this.

The committee that was appointed to select the winner knew from the beginning who would win the award for the most outstanding costume. It would go to the lovely lady in the white satin gown. When the signal was given for unmasking, Lottie slowly slipped off her mask, and the citizens of Bodie gasped. Lottie's partner immediately recognized her from his past, and he walked off the dance floor, leaving her standing alone. The "respectable" people could never allow someone who had been a prostitute to receive such a prestigious award — it just wouldn't be right. Two men whispered something into Lottie's ear and she ran from the ball in tears.

When Eli found out what had happened, he was like a wild bull and wanted to tear the town apart. Lottie, however, no longer cared. She knew there was no way the people would ever respect her. The Johls grew closer, keeping to themselves, their loneliness drawing

[1] **The Story of Bodie**, by Ella M. Cain

them together. Then one night Lottie became ill. Eli sent for a doctor who checked her over and ordered a prescription. Later, after Eli lovingly gave his wife the medication, she became violently ill. Within 24 hours Lottie was dead.

Everyone in Bodie started gossiping. They said it was sad that poor Mrs. Johl had committed suicide. Eli knew better. Although Lottie was unhappy, she would never have committed suicide. He demanded that an autopsy be performed. When the results were final, it was disclosed that Lottie had been given poison. Who would have poisoned Lottie? Not Eli, for he loved her. The officials decided her death was not intentional, it just happened. Besides, there were more important issues at hand, like where they would allow Eli to bury his wife.

The majority declared that since Mrs. Johl had been a fallen woman, she could not be buried in consecrated ground. A few stood up for Lottie. They felt that she had been a good faithful wife to Eli all the years they were married and deserved to be buried in the cemetery. Eli was filled with grief as well as anger. Why should these people, who never really knew his wife, decide where she was to be buried. Hadn't they hurt her enough! Finally a compromise was reached: Lottie Johl would be placed at the edge of the cemetery, just within the fence.

Eli Johl built a memorial for his Lottie. He erected a high wrought-iron fence around her grave; it was the most elaborate in the cemetery. *On Memorial Day he had a carpenter build a canopy that would cover her entire grave . . . and with his own hands Eli decorated it. He wrapped it first with buntin' (sic) of red, white and blue, with little flags here and there, and then entwined it with paper flowers of all descriptions. At the head of the grave he placed an enlarged picture of his darling. It was one in colors, showing her blonde hair, blue eyes, diamond earrings, and dress of lace.*[1]

Eli hoped the citizens of Bodie would visit his wife's grave and they did. First they came because they were curious, then because they were sad. The people finally realized the love Eli had had for his wife, perhaps a few were even sorry for the way they treated her. Many left with tears in their eyes, whether for Eli or Lottie, no one would ever know.

---

[1] **The Story of Bodie**, by Ella M. Cain

Eli continued to live alone in their house, visiting Lottie daily. Every Memorial Day he would decorate her grave and sit quietly beside it while curious visitors paused to see who was buried there. As the town declined, Eli decided to leave Bodie. He sold the cottage, where there was once so much love, and left the past behind.

Today, as the desolate wind blows over the desert, Lottie Johl sleeps on. Her tomb is a silent memory of a town that once boasted of the wickedest men and the wildest streets, in a place that is considered the last of the old-time mining camps.

The author would like to thank Jill Lachman, seasonal aide at Bodie State Historic Park, for her cooperation in obtaining dates and information about Lottie Johl, and Mrs. Helen Evans for allowing her mother's fascinating book, The Story of Bodie by Ella M. Cain, to be used as a reference guide and for short quotes.

* In 1964 Bodie became a California Historic Landmark and a National Historic Site.

The residence of Lottie and Eli Johl

After the fire of 1932, this building was used as a post office with Mrs. Mary McDonald presiding as the last postmistress of Bodie.

Courtesy of Bodie State Historic Park, Bodie, California
Photo: © Jill A. Lachman

Lottie Johl's painting in Bodie State Historic Park Museum

*Lottie's front room stove kept her warm during
Bodie's cold winter nights.*

The Grand Central Hotel in Bodie, California, Circa 1880

Lottie traveled to Bodie by Stagecoach in 1882. It took 36 hours to get to Bodie and cost $36.
The passengers left the stage in front of this fine hotel.

Courtesy of The Montana Historical Society, Helena, Montana

◆━━━━━━━━━━━━━━━━━━━━━━━━◆

"Chicago Joe" Hensley of Helena, Montana

Chapter 5

THE ENTREPRENEURS

A lthough the madams were among the early entrepreneurs, historians often fail to recognize their significant contributions to the Western economy. These enterprising women, who played an important role within their communities, were never invited to join or attend a commercial club. They were not accepted by society, and, in most cases, denied the protection of the law, due to their profession.

Collectively, their businesses employed the largest group of women on the frontier. They supplied a home for thousands of females who would have otherwise been forced to live on the streets.

The majority of the madams owned their own real estate, and all provided a considerable amount of revenue to their city or town. They paid property, school and county taxes, license fees and filled the pockets of corrupt officials and police officers. The society that did not respect these businesswomen, nonetheless expected them to donate generously to churches and local charities. Merchants, who profited off the ladies, overcharged them for liquor, food and personal goods. In order to run a successful business, with a substantial return, the western madam had to have a great deal of patience and more than the usual amount of business acumen. Josephine Airey, known as "Chicago Joe," was one of these women.

In 1858, at the young age of 14, a pretty girl named Mary Welch left her home in Ireland behind, to find a better life in America. Several weeks later, she arrived in New York with an Irish brogue, an empty pocketbook and a lot of ambition.

The first thing Mary did was change her name to the more

stylish Josephine Airey. The second thing she did was find work. Since she had little experience, she no doubt took a menial job. She eventually tired of New York, and a few years later Josephine moved on to Chicago, where she became a member of the demimonde. She was a hard working young woman, who was proficient at her profession, and in 1867, at the age of 23, Josephine boarded a train for the rich mining town of Helena, Montana.

Josephine brought three things with her from Chicago — her savings, experience, and the charm of the Irish. It was obvious there was money to be made in the rough town with its muddy streets and clapboard houses, so she invested in a piece of property on Wood Street. Her first business venture was a crude, one story hurdy-gurdy house, which became so profitable that three years later Josephine needed to expand.

Because she lacked the necessary capital, Josephine had to borrow from one of Helena's notorious lenders, Alex Lavenberg. His conditions were hard to meet, but the intrepid lady agreed to them. "Josephine Airey had mortgaged everything, including her underwear — *three dozen pair (of) underclothes.*"[1] Her new venture, however, was successful and she paid Lavenberg off six months before the note was due.

When the terrible fire of 1874 swept Helena, the majority of the buildings burned to the ground. Since few of the landowners had money to rebuild, Josephine was able to purchase their property, and at the age of 30, she became the largest land owner on Wood Street.

Four years later, Josephine Airey married James T. "Black Hawk" Hensley. Together, they built a fireproof stone dance hall and "The Red Light Saloon." With a new enterprise to manage, Josephine rented her properties to other businesses and became an influential landlady in Helena. At that time she acquired the sobriquet of "Chicago Joe."

For the next ten years, Joe took care of the profitable Red Light Saloon and her "ladies." In 1886, when the city fathers barred prostitution and declared hurdy-gurdy houses immoral, Joe boldly challenged the courts. She hired an attorney who defended her with a few brilliant words and a Webster's Dictionary. According to

[1] **Capitalists with Rooms**, Paula Petrik

Webster, a hurdy-gurdy was a mechanical device that resembled a hand organ. Since the music at the Red Light Saloon was provided by a three piece band, not a hurdy-gurdy, the case was thrown out of court. Joe was allowed to keep the doors of her saloon open.

As the population of Helena continued to grow more sophisticated, Joe decided she needed a new stylish business. She built a large, elaborate establishment named the "Coliseum," a combination theater and variety house, and began importing fresh, feminine talent from the East. The presence of these well-groomed, attractive ladies, and entertainers, made the Coliseum the most popular place in Helena — prostitution and bawdy amusement provided a handsome profit.

Joe's new Coliseum was elite. It had elegant furnishings and many amenities, including special boxes equipped with electric bells which were connected to the bar. An eager gentleman could order a fast drink, as well as a fast woman — the proprietress had thought of everything!

Chicago Joe had become an impressive woman. "Her theater was a success, generating a weekly payroll of $1,000 and more. She paid taxes on more than $200,000 worth of property."[1] Josephine, at the age of 44, was wealthy and powerful. Her donations to local charities were as large as her contributions to certain political candidates. She dressed in fashionable gowns, enjoyed luxurious furs, and wore expensive jewelry. Her lifestyle was flamboyant, and her many parties and balls were the talk of Helena.

However, the good life could not last forever. As Helena grew into a city of prominence and culture, the Coliseum lost its novelty and charm. In 1893 the financial panic, and eventual depression, put an end to prosperity and Josephine Hensley. She tried desperately to save her businesses, but lost everything except the Red Light Saloon. The notorious Chicago Joe and her husband moved into an apartment above the saloon and lived a quiet life.

On October 25, 1899, at the age of 55, the colorful Chicago Joe died of pneumonia. The citizens of Helena provided a large funeral and made long speeches about her accomplishments — and the young, uneducated Irish girl, who rose to fame and wealth, became

[1] **An Inning for Sin, Rex C. Meyers**, Montana Magazine

another page in the book of Helena's turbulent history.

———◆———

One of the most fascinating stories of the mid-1800s was that of Mary Ellen Pleasant, a lady of intrigue and mystery who was known to San Franciscans as "Mammy" Pleasant. Although many people called her a saint, others claimed she was a sinner. Maybe she was both —

Mary Ellen, a Georgia slave, was the daughter of a white man and a Haitian quadroon. She was a bright, attractive girl who had no trouble passing as a white child. At the age of ten she came to the attention of her owner and was sent to a convent to be educated; she never returned to the plantation. Mary Ellen became a part of the Underground Railroad and spent the next few years helping her people to escape from slavery.

During that time she met and married a wealthy abolitionist twice her age. He died a few years later leaving a small fortune. Following his death, Mary Ellen continued to work with the Underground and contributed a large amount of money to the "cause." Her skin was so light that she had to darken it with walnut stain to pass as black.

As Mary Ellen's involvement with the movement became well-known, she was forced to flee to New Orleans for safety, where she became a cook in a fashionable restaurant. Tales of California's rich gold fields filled the newspapers, and in 1852 Mary Ellen left New Orleans for the wealth of San Francisco. Her first job in the city was as a cook for two well-to-do bachelors. Mary Ellen's cooking became a popular attraction and the shrewd woman used the remainder of her money to open an elegant "boarding" house.

At that point in her life, the attractive lady could have easily passed as a white female. She was already used to assuming disguises and was clever enough to be successful at the art of deception. Mary Ellen, however, chose to take her place in society as a member of her own race and became known as "Mammy" Pleasant.

Her boarding house was a popular enterprise, and she soon added several beautiful, young women to her staff who became known as her "protégés." These girls dressed in the latest fashions and, through Mammy's influence, the majority of them either married wealthy men or became involved in profitable alliances. They all remained under Mammy's control, and she manipulated their lives whenever it would benefit her businesses.

Since her first boarding house was so successful, Mary Ellen added more houses throughout the city. Her clientele were rich and influential and her attractive ladies were willing to participate in an evening of pleasure. She often had special parties for important men. At one of these parties she met Thomas Bell, a wealthy investor, who became Mary Ellen's partner and "front man" for her many ventures.

With the help of Bell, Mary Ellen purchased her first rental properties on the Barbary Coast, an unsavory area, from which she collected high rents. She also invested in laundries, brothels, saloons and livery stables. As more and more penniless Negroes began arriving in San Francisco, she either hired them to work for her or found them employment as servants in wealthy households. In return, she demanded faithfulness and expected the ex-slaves to bring her the secrets of their employers.

Mary Ellen carefully set up a network of loyal spies throughout San Francisco. They kept her informed of every scandal or business deal. Powerful men began coming to Mammy for advice and she willingly gave it — always with an eye toward her own financial gain. Mary Ellen and Thomas Bell set up crooked business deals and ambitious schemes that made her rich and added to Bell's already considerable fortune. Within a few years the clever woman was able to sit in her home on Washington Street and manipulate the city.

Mary Ellen, however, did more than rule others. She gave of herself as well as her money. She was a strong civil rights advocate long before the movement existed and sent large checks to abolitionist, John Brown, who was attempting to free the slaves. No black person was ever turned away from her door empty-handed. On several occasions Mary Ellen was responsible for removing innocent girls from the houses of prostitution and helping them to lead a better life.

Shortly before her death, the October 13, 1895, San Francisco Examiner ran this story: "Neither creed, color, sex or condition in life ever had meaning for her when her intent once had been awakened. Her deeds of charity are as numerous as the gray hairs in her proud old head . . . *I want no compliments,* she said. *I can't abide by them. No matter what I have done; it has been little enough . . . I have frequently filled my buggy with fruits and turkeys — cooked, stuffed and uncooked — it was all the same, and taken them to churches and hospitals. I am a Catholic, but one church was the same as another to me. It was all for the cause."*

No two stories are alike when it came to Mary Ellen "Mammy" Pleasant. She was either an evil woman or a female Robin Hood. It is known that she and Thomas Bell built an elaborate mansion on Octavia Street, which for many years was called "The House of Evil." It was rumored that strange things, including voodoo, took place within its elegant walls. When Bell married Theresa Clingan, Mammy Pleasant remained in the house until his death in 1892, then moved into her own apartment.

As the years passed, Mammy Pleasant grew older in body, while her mind remained as active as ever. She had spun her spider's web for almost 50 years, and it slowly disintegrated around her. At the turn of the century, Mammy Pleasant claimed she was poverty ridden, and the courts found her an insolvent debtor. She died a few years later in 1904, at the age of 92. Whatever secrets Mammy Pleasant had, and no doubt she had many, went to the grave with the mysterious lady.

———◆———

In the early days, Seattle was a town of young unmarried males, with a ratio of two women for every 90 men. Most of the females over 15 years old were spoken for, or married, and there were no "old maids."

As thousands of single men poured into Seattle, with money to spend, and time to kill, it became a wide-open town where gambling, robberies and prostitution flourished. The high-class ladies lived in expensive hotels and the "girls" operated along " Skid Road."

The name Skid Road, a logging term, once meant a trail of

greased skids used by ox teams to haul logs to the sawmills. A "Skid Road" in any logging or sawmill town became the term for the district containing bordellos and saloons which catered to the needs of loggers and lumbermen. This was the world of Mary Ann Boyer.

There has been very little written about Mary Ann Boyer, Seattle's own "Madam Damnable." She was a diminutive lady, who stood less than five feet tall, and when aroused had a repertoire of profanity that would shock a hardened sinner.

Mary Ann was a friend of Doc Maynard, a man who was one of the key factors in the city's early growth. Doc, for unknown reasons, used his influence to establish her business and was instrumental in helping the feisty little "lady" to reach the top of her profession as Seattle's first madam. Her "house" stood on a point overlooking the Sound, and it has been shown in many old history books. Unfortunately, the owner's name was omitted due to her occupation.

Mary Ann's establishment resembled a Southern mansion which had been moved to the Pacific Northwest. It was a two-storied structure, built with square columns, an eight-foot front door and a magnificent verandah. At the rear of the house, near the kitchen, were several small cubicles such as those designed for Southern slaves — but there were no slaves in Seattle. In these small rooms, the "girls" provided necessary services for visiting gentlemen.

Although she was often referred to as a "demon in petticoats" and an "old dragon," Madam Damnable operated her business with finesse and discretion. She had a kind heart and was good to her ladies.

When Washington became a territory in 1853, its first legislative session was held in Madam Damnable's house. While in session, the "Queen of Sin" charged the members outrageous prices for food and lodging which were grudgingly paid. If a gentleman protested, the lady would hurl her favorite oaths at the man, often accompanied by a barrage of pots and pans.

Important dignitaries, who became guests at Madam Damnable's house, enjoyed her fine food and luxurious bedrooms. Most of the men had no idea of what went on in the small rooms near the kitchen, unless they responded with the appropriate answer to the question, "What is your pleasure?"

The madam's first floor parlor and upstairs bedrooms served the judiciary from Monday to Friday — on weekends, when the loggers came to town, they were available for more pleasurable pursuits. Sin and legislators' money made the little lady a fortune and Seattle famous.

As Seattle grew, many religious groups began a drive to remove prostitution from their midst. Madam Damnable's operation, however, was so unobtrusive and her clientele so respected, that the local residents left her alone. The little madam, with her large vocabulary, went on raking in the money and providing a necessary service.

The "Demon in Petticoats" operated until she passed away in the late 1860s. Her bawdy personality added a touch of color to Old Seattle, and her establishment had served the town well.

"CHICAGO JOE" DEAD

Mrs. Josephine Hensley, better known throughout Montana and other parts of the west as "Chicago Joe," died yesterday morning at 2:30 o'clock at her home on Wood Street . . . "Chicago Joe" was a woman of extraordinary strength of character. She and her place, in their time, were known far and wide throughout this western country. Her life in some respects was an eventful one. Most of it was spent in Helena at its most stirring period.

. . . In those days "Joe" herself presided nightly over the cashing of checks and the general business of the theater. She wore a flowing robe of heavy velvet, generally green or purple, with a pink-lined Elizabethan collar of enormous size, a wide golden, jewel-studded girdle around the immense expanse where her waist once was and jewels on every part of her dress where it was possible to place them. Thus attired and carefully painted and powdered she presented an imposing appearance as she swept along.

. . . "Chicago Joe" had her faults, but she was a woman of generous impulses, and she assisted many unfortunate women who came to her for help. In former days she contributed liberally to every public enterprise . . . She gave liberally also to charity. Although a hard master, she was always a generous one . . .

Her life was a checkered one. She suffered numerous losses from friends who sought her assistance and who generally failed to return the money she loaned. Several times she was robbed by her associates . . .

— Helena Daily Independent, October 26, 1899

Josephine Hensley's funeral took place in the cathedral of the Sacred Heart, she was buried in the Catholic cemetery.

Mr. Hamilton

Mr. Hamilton, also known as "The Duke," often worked for
Chicago Joe and the other madams of Helena, Montana.

Lillie

Annette

◆———————————————◆

Both Lillie and Annette were employed by Chicago Joe.

Jackie

Jackie was about 15 when she began her career as a prostitute.
Many girls entered the profession at an even younger age.

*Courtesy of the California State Library, Sacramento, California,
a San Francisco Chronicle photo, July 9, 1899*

◆————————————————————————◆

"Mammy" Pleasant, San Francisco's lady of mystery

LIFE STORY OF MAMMY PLEASANT

"Mammy" Pleasance (sic), the colored woman who has occupied a unique position in San Francisco for nearly five decades, is slowly succumbing to the weight of her years... It seems that the lamp is about burned out ... and slowly but surely the old "Mammy" is approaching the end of the road.

The life of this woman has been one of intense activity since the days of her childhood. She has always been at work, and those whom she has befriended now gratefully acknowledge that her greatest efforts have been exerted unselfishly in behalf of others. Her expertise in this city and state since her arrival would form one of the most interesting volumes that California has ever known. Safely locked in her loyal breast are the secret histories of many of the prominent families of the Coast. She has supplied the ladder upon which more than one proud woman and ambitious man have climbed to wealth and social position. Her purse has ever been open to aid the needy and unfortunate.

— San Francisco Examiner, October 13, 1895

MAMMY PLEASANT

Mammy Pleasant, the mild-mannered old Southern mammy of romantic newspaper writers with her spotless white apron and neckerchief and her bunch of keys and her general air of contrition for being so good, has been for many years the most discussed woman in San Francisco.

She has been called a pauper, then a millionaire, a devout Catholic, a Methodist, a leader among the Baptists, the essence of truth, and a perjurer, a friend of the poor, and a woman who turned every human passion and foible to her own advantage, and used the people that she chose to associate with as so many pawns on a chess board.

A woman with wonderful persuasive powers, and something very like a hypnotic influence over the members of her own sex, she has been placed in dozens of positions of trust... Every property of this character that Mammy has controlled has faded into thin air... charges of mal-administration have been housed against her... The Taylor estate was left in Mammy's charge . . . six months later she (Mrs. Taylor) and her four children were turned out of the house . . .

— San Francisco Chronicle, July 9, 1899

Courtesy of Walt Almquist's Murray Museum, Murray, Idaho

Walt Almquist's Murray Museum has been in possession of this photo since the early 1950s and has searched extensively for others. After over 40 years of careful photo and clothing analyzation, the museum has officially announced that the image is of Maggie Hall, aka Molly b' Dam.

Chapter 6

MOLLY b' DAM

E very mining camp and cow town has its own legend of the beautiful prostitute with a heart of gold, and Molly b' Dam could easily be the prototype for them all. Although it has been over a century since she last rode her high-spirited stallion through the doors of a Murray saloon, and ordered "Drinks for the house," the lovely lady is as much alive today as she was in the past — just ask any old-timer of North Idaho's Coeur d'Alenes.

Molly b' Dam entered this world as Maggie Hall in Dublin, Ireland on December 26, 1853. Both her English Protestant father and Irish Catholic mother were well-educated, and they provided a better than average home for the sparkling little girl. Maggie was carefully raised and received a fine education. She was a lively outgoing child who made friends easily and often was considered to be a non-conformist.

Maggie grew into an exceptionally beautiful young woman. She was five feet six inches tall, with golden blonde hair, expressive blue eyes and a contagious laugh. Her shapely figure was admired by women and desired by men. Although Maggie received many proposals of marriage, she always managed, in her own charming way, to discourage the eager young men. Her restless spirit seemed to be constantly seeking new adventures, but in the 1870s Ireland had little to offer a girl like Maggie Hall.

At the age of 20, Maggie decided to journey to America, a land she felt would fulfill her dreams. Although her distraught mother and father fought against the move, Maggie had made up her mind. She packed her clothing and a few personal possessions and left both her doting parents and the shores of Ireland behind.

The trip across the Atlantic was a joy to the young woman. Her anticipation and excitement of a new life were stronger than any fear she might have felt. As the New York skyline came into view, Maggie was overwhelmed by the large city — she knew that it was hers to conquer. The lovely Maggie Hall, however, was wrong.

New York could be a cruel city. Although Maggie was well educated and spoke English, with a bit of an Irish brogue, she could not find employment. As her money began to disappear, Maggie decided she would accept whatever was offered. She was soon working at a saloon as a barmaid. Maggie's sharp wit and natural charm made her popular with the men and her strong Catholic upbringing let them know she was a no-nonsense girl.

By the end of her first year, Maggie had earned the respect and love of the customers, barmaids and saloon owner. Although she had learned to drink her whiskey straight, Maggie was never known to be a heavy drinker. She was happy and busy exploring the city of New York. All of that changed, however, on a cold winter evening when a well-dressed young man, of obvious means, entered the saloon. He was the handsomest man Maggie had ever seen and, like thousands of women before her, Maggie Hall immediately fell in love with a stranger.

The man, who was named Burdan, also appeared to be attracted to Maggie's obvious charms. On his third visit to the bar, he proposed marriage to the unsophisticated young woman. Maggie, who had found that the handsome stranger was the son of a wealthy family, and also a bit of a womanizer, let her heart speak for her and accepted his proposal. They were married that night, but it was not the kind of marriage Maggie had always dreamed of. Instead of a Catholic ceremony, with a priest, she was married by a sleepy Justice of the Peace.

When Maggie became Mrs. Burdan, she also had to change her name to Molly because Maggie was too common. Then Mr. Burdan told her their marriage must be kept a secret. It seemed his income was a remittance from his parents, and without their approval, he would be penniless. So Molly Burdan began her new life married to a stranger without the blessing of her church.

The couple moved into Burdan's expensive apartment where Molly lived a life of luxury and ease, but only for a few months.

When Burdan's father found his son had married a barmaid, he discontinued the allowance. Without an income the Burdans were forced to move from apartment to apartment to avoid paying rent. Molly's husband had never worked, nor did he intend to. She wanted to return to her old job in the saloon, but Mr. Burdan wouldn't allow it —he had other plans for Molly.

Although Burdan was without funds, he continued to spend his time in saloons and gambling houses. His male friends constantly visited the Burdans and all desired the beautiful Molly. One night Molly's husband came to her with a desperate look upon his face and asked her to do what no self-respecting woman would ever do — sell her body to another man. Molly's life was shattered. She had never been with any man except Burdan, and she was a devout Catholic who knew the Church would never forgive her.

When Molly refused, Burdan put his head in her lap and begged her to save him — and Molly finally submitted to her husband's wishes — for she loved him. Over the next few weeks, Burdan brought many men home for Molly to entertain. She quietly did as she was told, but her heart was broken and her love for Burdan began to disappear.

Molly went to confession and was warned to discontinue following her husband's wishes. The next time she went to confess the same sins, she was not only denied forgiveness, she was also denied the sanctity of the Church. Molly Burdan had been formally excommunicated — and she believed her soul was damned forever. From that day on, Molly obviously considered herself to be a sinner, because as such she continued her life.

At the age of 24 Molly Burdan left her husband and traveled to the cities, mining camps and cow towns of the West. She visited San Francisco for a brief period, then moved on to Oregon. Molly was seen in Chicago, Virginia City, Nevada, and the Dakota Territory. As she traveled, Molly became skilled at her new profession and a sought-after prostitute. The price for her favors was high and she had acquired an expensive wardrobe which included furs and exquisite jewelry. Although she had success and money, Molly's spirit was as restless as ever.

In 1884 when Molly was 30, she read a circular describing the rich gold strike in the Coeur d'Alenes. She immediately boarded a train heading for the Idaho Territory. Calamity Jane was also traveling on the train for the same reason as Molly — a share of the gold. When the two ladies met, they decided Murray wasn't large enough for both of them and Calamity returned to Deadwood, Dakota Territory.

Molly left the train at Thompson Falls, Montana, where she purchased a strong horse and joined a pack train on its way to Murray, Idaho. They had to travel through deep snow over treacherous Thompson Pass. "Those who could not afford the price of a horse strapped their belongings on their backs or on a toboggan, dragging them behind them. The journey by pack train took a whole day, in the time when a whole day meant a whole day!"[1]

As the train moved along at a slow, steady pace a blizzard started, and soon everyone was struggling, especially those on foot. A mother, carrying her small child, was attempting to keep up with the rest of the group when she stumbled and fell. Molly got down off her horse and put both of them up on her saddle with her. She noticed that the woman and child were not dressed for a blizzard and were freezing. When a battered shelter appeared, Molly pulled away from the train, took off her own fur coat and wrapped them in it. She told the train to move on without her, and the three of them spent the long, cold night huddled together in the crude shelter.

When the pack train arrived in Murray, word quickly spread of the beautiful woman who had stayed behind to help a mother and her child. No one expected to see any of them again. The next day, however, the town was surprised when Molly and her charges came galloping down the street. Molly handed the child down and someone helped the woman. People came from all directions to welcome the new arrivals, and Molly ordered a cabin and warm food for the woman and child. She requested the bill to be brought to her.

As Molly took a deep breath and looked around, she saw the face of a rollicking, young Irish man with a twinkle in his eyes. His name was Phil O'Rourke, a man who was to become her friend and confidant for the rest of her life. When O'Rourke asked Molly her name she replied "I'm Molly Burdan," but he misunderstood her

---

[1] **The Legend of Molly b' Dam'**, Deborah H. Mellon

and responded in his heavy Irish brogue . . . "Well now, fur the life o'me, I'd never o' thought it. Molly b' Dam."[1] And so the legend of Molly b' Dam began in a small town called Murray and spread throughout the West.

As the local citizenry gathered around to admire the high-spirited lady who sat proudly upon her horse, Molly announced she wouldn't be needing a hotel. She wanted cabin number one. In Murray, as throughout the West, cabin number one was reserved for the madam of the red light district. No one batted an eye or said a word. Phil O'Rourke gallantly helped Molly off her horse and carried her luggage to the cabin she requested. Molly knew she was welcome, and for the first time in her life her restless spirit was at peace. Molly Burdan had finally found her home.

Molly was happy in Murray. She was kind to her girls and the locals were kind to her. She was constantly feeding hungry families and anyone who was down on their luck knew that Molly b' Dam would provide warm clothing and shelter. Although she lived in luxury, Molly never hesitated to climb to a mountain cabin to nurse a sick prospector. She even began attending church services, but not in the Catholic Church — she could never return to her own faith.

Shortly after Molly's arrival, a miner known as "Lightnin" came to town with his pouch full of gold. He had two things on his mind, whiskey and women. As he went from saloon to saloon, the rough miner got roaring drunk and headed for Molly's place to bed with one, or more, of her girls. The next day when he awakened and reached for his pouch of gold, he found it was missing. Lightnin' went into a rage and accused Molly of stealing his gold. Molly indignantly told Lightnin' that she had no control over her girls, although she knew they were not noted for their honesty. The man had visited many cabins, and she had no way of knowing who might have taken it. The dejected miner knew in his heart that Molly was right. He bought a small outfit on credit and returned to his diggings.

Three months later, Lightnin's partner came to town and let it be know that Lightnin' was dying. Molly was worried and upset. She gathered food, bedding and medical supplies and set off for

[1] **The Legend of Molly b' Dam'**, Deborah H. Mellon

Lightnin's cabin to nurse him back to health. When she arrived he was semiconscious and burning with fever. Molly spent several days caring for the man until he was better. The first person he saw when he opened his eyes was Molly b' Dam. When he asked her what she was doing there, Molly threw him his pouch of gold. She had told her girls that Lightnin' was ill and needed his poke, and someone had placed it upon her dresser. Whoever had stolen the pouch couldn't keep it knowing a man was dying — there was honor, even among prostitutes.

Molly was a bit of a comedienne. She was comfortable everywhere she went and had a keen sense of humor. In her book, "The Legend of Molly b' Dam'," Deborah Mellon wrote: "Molly also had a fun side to her, and she played this up as much as modern day Robin Williams shocks and astounds his audiences. She was a woman of first class taste and demeanor . . . everything about her spoke aces." [1]

One of the well-known stories about Molly concerned her unique way of taking a bath while getting rich. It was said "she hit the jackpot from both sides of the curtain." Molly knew when the big cleanups from the mines were due, and she would have her own "big cleanup bath." This popular, highly advertised event took place in Paradise Alley, behind her establishment. Molly would come out of her cabin, blonde curls piled high, and draperies flowing, dragging a large tub which she filled with water. Her chatter was lively and full of ribald wit as she encouraged "the boys" to dig into their pockets and cover her tub with gold. As soon as the bottom of the tub was covered, off would come her clothing and into the tub went the curvaceous Molly. While she sat on the gold, her glib remarks and risqué chatter kept the party moving at a fast pace. Occasionally a lucky miner was allowed to scrub the lady's back — that is if the price was right.

In 1886 a stranger arrived in Murray burning with a fever. He drove his horse up to the saloon, drank a pint of whiskey, and dropped dead. The stranger had the dreaded smallpox and the whole town was at risk. There was no escape and soon people began dying by the dozen. They tried to hide in their houses, hoping it would pass them by, but it never did. There was one ineffectual

---

[1]**The Legend of Molly b' Dam'**, Deborah H. Mellon

doctor in town and no hospital, and everyone was terrified.

After a few days, it was apparent that no one knew what to do, so Molly decided to call a town meeting. As the people gathered outside the court house, Molly began to lash out at them with a fury they had never seen. According to witnesses she said, "You don't lick anything by running away from it, or hiding your heads under your pillows! You hole up in your homes or rooms, thinking maybe this won't find you, while your friends and neighbors are dying off alone, unattended . . . Well, I'm not afraid. There are a dozen sick men up there in my part of town and me and my girls are doing what we can for them . . ."

Molly's impassioned speech brought the town to life and gave them a direction in which to go. O'Rourke joined her and together they helped clear out the hotels and fill them with the sick. Molly and her girls became nurses. The one doctor began to help and others joined in. They administered to the ill in the makeshift hospitals, treating them with all known medications.

It has been said that Molly b' Dam worked tirelessly. She was everywhere, nursing patients until she could no longer stand. She barely ate and didn't take time to even change her clothing. As the weeks dragged by, there were less and less patients and soon the daily procession to the cemetery ceased. The town had survived — but Molly was never to be the same.

In October of 1887, Molly became weary and listless and soon developed a constant fever and hacking cough. O'Rourke was the first person to notice her tiredness and loss of weight, but when he asked Molly to rest, she gave him her usual bawdy answer and shook her head. O'Rourke, however, knew his friend was very sick and in his concern asked some of the women to look in on Molly. They willingly began to visit her and soon realized she was seriously ill.

By November she became bed-ridden with a constant fever and a cough that never stopped. The women of Murray kept a 24-hour vigil at Molly's bedside and the doctor diagnosed her illness as consumption, a disease for which there was no cure. As Molly continued to worsen, Phil O'Rourke sat in quiet prayer by her side, and on January 17, 1888, Molly b' Dam was gone.

News of Molly's death spread throughout the mountains and the Protestant ministers, who had been visiting Molly daily, asked the Catholic priest to give the woman absolution. When he refused, they made arrangements for her funeral.

On that sad day every blind was drawn on every window. The miners' sluice boxes and diggins' remained silent and all the saloons closed their doors. Thousands of people came from all over the surrounding area to bid farewell to the lady who had brought gaiety and love to their community and touched their hearts as no other ever had.

The services were simple and the Methodist minister's eulogy was spoken from his heart. Molly had known she was dying, and before the end came she requested a simple wooden marker with the name "Maggie Hall," which was also her mother's name, to be inscribed deeply in the wood — it was done as she wished.

Today, stories of the prostitute with the heart of gold live on. In Murray's few remaining saloons, words from her song, "The Legend of Molly b' Dam'," fill the air and every August there is a two-day celebration in honor of Murray's most illustrious personality.

The author would like to thank Deborah H. Mellon for her delightful book, The Legend of Molly b' Dam' *and the use of her notes and brief quotes, and the University of Idaho for their courtesy and cooperation in locating old records and newspaper articles about Molly Burdan.*

THE EULOGY FOR MOLLY b' DAM

This Eulogy was found clipped to Molly's death
record in the Murray Courthouse.

*... Maggie Hall has gone from our midst, but she will
never be forgotten, living forever in our hearts a
woman so strong, so forthright that only her good
deeds will be remembered. Generous to a fault with
her worlds goods, and with her bodily strength, she
was one in whom no sacrifice was too great. She was
a ministering angel to the sick and suffering when
exposure of illness laid men low. Neither snow nor
heat kept her from an unfortunate's bedside, and these
kind acts have been recorded in the Book of Books to
her credit, overbalancing the debt side.*

*... She flashed like a diamond among us, until she
herself was laid low by a lingering illness which
brought her untimely end in a humble cabin which
was home to her.*

*... And to the credit of Him in whom she placed her
trust, her last days were made comfortable, if not
happy; and her every want was readily met. To the
lasting credit of our Christian ladies it must be said
that they were not unmindful of the want of the sufferer
in her long illness; and whatever could be done by
them was done without ostentation, in the pure and
noble spirit.*

*... God rest your soul, Maggie Hall, through eternity.
Amen.*

Molly b' Dam's tombstone in Murray, Idaho.

Courtesy of The University of Idaho, Moscow, Idaho

Murray, Idaho, 1890

◆━━━━━━━━━━━━━━━━━━━━━━◆

*The life of the Western prostitute often was
one of degradation and despair.*

Chapter 7

A LITTLE AFFECTION, PLEASE

◆ ────────────────────────────────── ◆

I t has been said that social disease and unwanted pregnancy were the occupational hazards of prostitution, but in reality it was loneliness. The "soiled dove," by her own choice, cut herself off from her family and was isolated by society. Her rights as a citizen were also removed. Since she worked outside of the law she had no protection. If the woman had children, they, too, were considered outcasts. Her constant moves from one location to another and many sexual partners, or "husbands," dramatically affected her children's lives. It was a harsh world for them, where existence was a constant struggle.

The daughter of a prostitute often followed in her mother's footsteps. She was usually illiterate and had little contact with the outside world. Prostitution was familiar to her and she did what was natural. The majority of these girls entered the profession at an early age. By the time they were in their mid-20s, most of them had become offensive alcoholic, drug users. They lived a life of violence with little, if any, affection. On July 7, 1876, *The Rocky Mountain News* published the following account of two young girls who were used as prostitutes:

A beastly woman was before Justice Whitemore yesterday on a charge of harboring young girls for immoral purposes, and the evidence — which is unfit for publication — showed that the woman, as well as the males associated with her in this wicked business deserve to be lynched. The men having not yet been arrested. The woman, who gave her name as Mary Gallagan, but who is also known as 'Adobe Moll,' was committed for trial at the district court, the crime being beyond the jurisdiction of a justice. One of the two girls decoyed into Moll's den was the little colored girl who some years since lost both her arms and one leg by being run over by the cars. She is about thirteen years old, and her companion, a white girl is only eleven . . .

In many instances it was the girl's own mother who forced her into prostitution. The June 7, 1877, *Territorial Enterprise* in Virginia City, Nevada, tells of a 13 year old girl who was rescued from the brothel of Nellie Sayers. She had been coerced by her mother to drink alcohol and receive men, or have her throat cut. Nellie Sayers reputedly kept children in her "house," and willingly supplied her customers with little girls.

Following her removal from the house of prostitution, the child said she hated what she had been forced to do and begged the police to protect her from a woman she accused as being an unnatural mother. The newspaper column reported: *The girl was very small for her age and quite fragile. She says she had not had anything to eat for two days, living constantly on the liquor she had been forced to drink. There is no doubt that the girl is telling the truth.*

Although the average prostitute provided as well as she could for her children, there were times when she was no longer able to care for them. At this point, other prostitutes would attempt to help. In most cases, however, the children were placed in a poor farm or an orphanage. Prominent citizens traditionally ignored these heart-breaking situations.

Women in prostitution were used to rejection. Their husbands, or lovers, were a sorry assortment of frontier gamblers, criminals, saloon keepers or pimps. These men used their women for support and helped push them down even lower in the social structure. They abused the prostitutes both verbally and physically, and often went as far as to murder them.

Mollie Forrest, at the age of 22, was one of these unfortunate victims. She was murdered by her husband, Joe Scott, a man with an unsavory reputation and ugly temper. The couple had arrived in Butte, Montana, a few days before Mollie started working in a dance hall and saloon. Somehow Mollie angered Scott. He dragged her off the dance floor, and took her above to her prostitute's room where he pulled his gun from its holster and blew half of the beautiful Mollie's face away. Although she was his only means of support, Scott had killed her in a fit of passion while stunned witnesses watched in horror. There were many Mollie Forrests.

The prostitute's friends and colleagues were also uncouth. She was caught in a situation over which she had little control, with no one to turn to for help. Most of the fallen women were explosive and unpredictable. They would drink to excess or get high on opiates, then unleash their anger and frustration upon each other. In time of illness or death, however, these same women willingly assumed full responsibility for the care of their associate. When death struck, the women helped to bury their own. Having so little for themselves, they still provided a decent burial — for all dreaded going to a lonely potter's field.

All of the soiled doves knew their careers were short-lived and few, if any, made plans for a better future. They spent their money on worthless things of little value. Some became so tired of being abused by men that they turned to another woman for tenderness or love. Those who once believed the life of a fancy lady would be filled with thrills and excitement found themselves, instead, looking at a foreboding, barren future. Many became so tired of being victimized, they took it upon themselves to end it by suicide.

Lottie Ables Pickett was one of these women. She was an unstable person who appeared to be running from something, always driven on to new scenes and new ventures as she traveled the mining towns of Montana. When Lottie arrived in Helena in the 1870s, she was given the nickname of "Sorrel Mike," after a race horse that was brought to the territory about the same time. Although there are no photos of Lottie, it was said she was an attractive dancer and prostitute with dark auburn hair and a gentle demeanor.

Whatever Sorrel Mike felt inside, she kept to herself and presented a gay front to her friends and colleagues. There is no evidence of a pimp in her life, so Lottie no doubt worked alone, occasionally taking a temporary job in a high-class brothel. She was admired by many men and obviously had no problem satisfying their needs. No one, however, knew what private despair filled Lottie's heart. Perhaps she became tired of selling her body and wanted a love that would provide tenderness for herself.

She eventually moved to Butte — Lottie was still running. On August 28, 1879, Dr. C. P. Hough of Butte was called at 2:00 a.m. to *rescue a fair lady from the jaws of death.* This wasn't the first time a doctor had been summoned to help Lottie Ables, for she had been on the verge of death, by her own hand, more than once already. It began in Helena, and in Butte her death wish continued.

The Butte Daily Miner reported: *The doctor promptly repaired to the bedside of the sufferer whom he found far gone in the stupor preceding death by opium poisoning. The lady, Mrs. Pickett, by her legal name, sometimes styled Sorrel Mike by the undevout, became a blushing bride about two weeks ago.*

Lottie had married a man she barely knew; one who did not come to her as a loving husband. Instead, he was a saloon keeper who expected his new wife to continue on with her profession, thus adding to his income. The newspaper continued on with: *It is likely that the felicity of the married state was found by experience to fall short of her girlish imagination . . . During Tuesday, to alleviate the pangs of a toothache, she had partaken of laudanum so liberally that in the evening, when the hour arrived for her to repair to the saloon where her husband earns an honest living by looking on while his wife dances, it was with great difficulty that she could be sufficiently aroused.*

Lottie performed that evening, but returned to her lodging determined to end her life. She swallowed the remaining laudanum in the vial. Relief was not to be granted, however, for Lottie continued to live on, only to try another time.

One year later Lottie was in the news again. On July 31, 1880, *The Butte Daily Miner* dutifully reported: *Sorrel Mike made up her mind the other day to go and be an angel, and with that intent, swallowed an overdose of morphine.* It would appear that to the newspaper, Lottie was an object of ridicule!

Following the latest suicide attempt, her husband vanished and she moved into a small house with her sister. It wasn't long before Lottie had a new lover and new problems. The couple quarreled constantly and once again Sorrel Mike attempted suicide, only this time she was successful. Her sister returned home to find Lottie lying on the floor with a bullet in her abdomen. At first Lottie claimed she had been shot by a man. Later, when she knew death was near, she admitted that she had pulled the trigger. The newspaper reported Lottie's age as being 30 years old; other records show she was only 22 at the time of her death. Either way, it was a very young age for such an unhappy life.

Not all fallen women were like Lottie Ables Pickett; many had the courage to stand up and fight the hand fate had dealt them. Maria Virginia Slade was one of these women. Her love for the infamous Jack Slade was all consuming — it became her life.

The high-spirited Virginia Slade arrived in Virginia City, Montana, in 1863. Her past, like that of the other shady ladies, was obscure. Some said she had been a hurdy-gurdy girl, others a gambling woman, but all agreed she had once been a lady of negotiable virtue. It is not known how or when Slade met his wife, the most popular story being that she had saved his life during a gambling brawl. One thing was obvious — Virginia was happy to be the wife of Jack Slade, for it is doubtful she had ever been loved before.

Virginia was a talented young woman who blended easily into the wide-open town. She was an excellent cook, fine seamstress and considered the handsomest woman in the Northern Rockies. Her tall, buxom figure, flashing eyes and dark raven hair attracted men from near and far, but Virginia's heart belonged to only one man — Jack Slade. This man, who she adored, had saved her from the sordid life she had once been forced to lead.

Slade was a little, red-faced man with a schizophrenic personality. He was a hard working freighter when sober and wild demon when drunk. Although it was rumored that Slade had killed 26 men, there was no proof that it was true. As a member of the Vigilantes, he was the idol of his followers and the terror of his enemies. Jack Slade appeared to be many things, and spent his life attempting to live up to the legends people created about him.

He was fond of his wife, and built her a comfortable rock house eight miles from Virginia City in the peaceful Meadow Valley. Virginia, who had never owned a home before, filled it with elegant furnishings which were brought in from Salt Lake City. The couple

◆————————————————————————————————◆

Maria Virginia Slade, the wife of the notorious Jack Slade

This rare photograph of Virginia Slade, from the Timothy Gordon Collection in Missoula, Montana, has not appeared in any previous publication.

settled down to share their lives and love for each other. They both enjoyed company and when Slade was sober, Virginia entertained their many friends with gourmet dinners and her warm personality.

The Slades also enjoyed dancing, at which Virginia excelled. She was always the pride of her husband as well as the most sought-after partner on the dance floor. While the other women wore simple cotton dresses, Virginia appeared in long, flowing silk gowns which she created with her own hands. Although she was easily the most popular woman at these affairs, Virginia never angered the other wives. She was a respected member of the community.

They both shared a love of horses. Virginia owned a black stallion named "Billy Boy," while Slade rode "Old Copper Bottom," who never failed to get him home, drunk or sober. The neighbors would often see the Slades riding together through the valley in the last of the evening's rays.

It was hard being the wife of Jack Slade. Virginia never knew where he was and she prayed daily for his safety. Whether Slade was on a drunken spree, or away on business, Virginia patiently waited in her rock house. She could tell by the sound of Old Copper Bottom's hooves if Slade had had too much to drink. On these occasions she lovingly helped him down from his horse, put him tenderly to bed, and sat by his side until he awoke. In Virginia's eyes, Slade could do no wrong.

She was not aware that Slade was in trouble with the law, or that the Vigilante committee had expelled him due to his drunkenness and danger to public safety. Slade had never been arrested for homicide or for an infraction of the law in Montana, save disturbing the peace.[1]

On March 8, 1864, the night before Slade was to meet his fate, a low, moaning wind began blowing throughout the valley. Virginia sat by her fireplace, anxiously awaiting the return of her husband, a pot of stew warming on the stove. On this particular evening, she felt more than the usual amount of concern. Slade had been due hours before. Although he seldom came home on time, there was something different about this particular night. As the darkness began to turn into dawn, Virginia started to pace the floor, wringing

---

[1] **Vigilante Woman**, by Virginia Rowe Towle

her hands. The wind had increased to a howl and tree branches tapped against the rock house. She peered out of the window, but there was no sign of Old Copper Bottom and no dear husband to help off his horse.

On that same night, Slade had been warned to return home and sober up, or there would be hell to pay. Being Jack Slade, however, he refused. The matter was taken before the assembly and the verdict was death by hanging. Slade's best friend, Jim Kiskadden, had pleaded in vain for banishment from the territory, not a lynching. When he saw there was no hope for Slade, he sent a message to Virginia.

As she sat and waited, Virginia had no way of knowing Slade's luck had run out, or that before the night was over he would be on his knees begging for mercy — mercy he never received.

When Virginia received the message, she saddled Billy Boy, and, distracted with love and fear, set out to save the object of her undivided affection. "With all the skill of an experienced equestrienne she urged the great horse up the heavy grade to the mountain top . . . The road was steep and rocky, dangerous at high speed. But she did not hesitate. Down the declivity she plunged regardless of danger to herself and horse . . . The multitude saw her coming at breakneck speed, her raven tresses blown by the strong wind"[1]

Despite her haste, Virginia had arrived too late — Slade was dead and her life as well as his was over. The last words upon his lips had been: "O, my dear wife." It was said his friends wept bitterly. Had Virginia arrived in time, she might have been able to save her husband. She was an expert shot and the people respected her.

Virginia bravely faced the unruly mob, and with tears streaming down her cheeks, she sobbed: "Why, oh, why didn't one of you shoot him and not let him endure the shame of being hanged? If I had been here, I would have done it. No dog's death should come to such a man. He did not deserve to die on the scaffold."[2] Then she flung herself upon her husband's lifeless body.

From that day forward, Virginia felt hatred for the people of Montana. She purchased a zinc coffin and preserved his remains in alcohol. He was temporarily buried across from the rock house,

[1] **The Montana Magazine of History**, Volume III, January, 1953
[2] **Vigilante Woman**, by Virginia Rowe Towle

where she could look out at the site. Later, Virginia had Slade's remains taken to Salt Lake City and interred in the Old Mormon Cemetery. She did not want her husband to rest among his enemies.

During her long months of grief, Jim Kiskadden became Virginia's constant companion, and eventually her husband. Their marriage, however, was a disaster, for no man could ever replace Jack Slade. Her body would always ache for his embrace and the touch of his lips. It was almost more than she could endure. Virginia left both Kiskadden and Montana behind — she no longer cared what happened.

The high-spirited, handsome woman, who had once been a loving, decent wife, returned from whence she came. She was discovered a few years later running a brothel — her life had come full circle. Virginia died shortly thereafter, alone, with nothing of value, save the memories of Jack Slade, which she would carry with her throughout eternity.

Years later, Slade's associates said they believed he did not commit a single act that was not justified by the circumstance provoking it.

◆

Although Lady Luck dealt Mollie Forrest, Lottie Ables Pickett and Virginia Slade a losing hand in the game of life, there was nothing more pathetic than the older prostitute who had lost her beauty and charm. She knew men no longer desired her; they only visited to fulfill a need. These women became even more dependent upon alcohol or opiates to ease their pain. Many left the larger cities, drifting to the barren frontier communities.

This move, however, may not have been to their advantage, as the end of the trail for a frontier prostitute was the "Hog Ranch." These miserable establishments were located along major thoroughfares such as the Bozeman Trail and the Cheyenne to Deadwood Stage Route. They came at a time when men were plentiful and women were scarce. Although the hog ranch provided a little diversion for the males, there was little affection for the females employed there.

These "dens of iniquity" offered cheap liquor, gambling and women. The buildings were not fancy. They ranged from sod huts and dugouts to more elaborate concrete shacks. The clientele consisted of cowboys, mule skinners, bullwackers and soldiers. The shady lady's status was governed mainly by her customer and the men these women served were just about at the bottom. Since soldiers earned about $13 a month, it would appear these soiled doves had reached the lowest rung of their profession.

On a daily basis, these women dealt with drunks, gunfighters and killings. They were a tough group who were not bedecked in silks and satins. The majority were unattractive and well past their prime, wearing clothing that consisted of bedraggled costumes from better days and old soldiers' uniforms.

In 1877, a Lt. John G. Bourke visited the hog ranch at Fort Laramie and wrote in a letter: *Three miles (from Fort Laramie) there was a nest of ranches. Cuhy and Scoffey's and Wright's, tenanted by as hardened and deprived a set of witches as could be found on the face of the globe . . . Each of these establishments was equipped with a run of the worst kind and each contained from three to half dozen Cyprians, virgins whose lamps were always burning brightly in expectancy of the coming of the bridegroom, and who lured to destruction soldiers of the garrisons. In all my experience I have never seen a lower, more beastly set of people of both sexes.*[1]

It was in this hog ranch, west of Fort Laramie, that the notorious Calamity Jane reputedly worked for a brief period. Several historical books and newspapers show Calamity was at the ranch in 1875, and again later in her life. She was a tough woman who often was the consort of soldiers, teamsters, bullwhackers and other disreputable men. Calamity used to boast that she was thrown out of a brothel in Bozeman, Montana, "for being a low influence on the inmates." It was said by saloon keepers that Calamity was part of the overhead of the saloons she frequented.

Although Calamity Jane has been described as an outlaw, liar, gambler and prostitute, there was another side to her story. She was also a kind, generous woman who willingly helped during a disaster or epidemic.

Calamity's childhood was not like that of the other children. Her mother, Charlotte, was a bold, flamboyant woman with a love for alcohol and men. Calamity's father was an unsuccessful man in

---

[1] **Record Times**, Wheatland, Wyoming, February 10, 1982

awe of his wife — who was referred to as "The toast of half the barrooms and Indian fighters from Walla Walla to Dodge City." As a small girl, Calamity grew up unsupervised, running with a rowdy pack of boys who taught her to down raw whiskey without coughing. At the age of 12, she would stand in the barroom doors and laugh at coarse jokes she didn't understand. Calamity's lessons of life came from brothels, dance halls and opium dens. Her dreams for the future were to run with the husky frontiersmen.

By the time Calamity was 15, she had become a rough-mannered young woman with her mother's coppery hair and an appetite for bawdy pleasures. She could use a 30-foot bullwhacker's whip, drive a team, and ride a horse as well as any man. Calamity preferred the open plains and the rough towns of the West. She wore teamster's clothing, imitated their swagger and laughed with sheer abandon at obscene stories. Calamity also shared her blanket with many men — she had a constant need for masculine companionship and was considered a good-natured camp trollop. While the perfumed, fancy ladies charged for their favors, Calamity bestowed hers free of charge — unless she needed the money.

At the age of 24, Calamity was a confirmed alcoholic who supported herself by freighting to the different camps with her bull team. The only women friends she had were in the red light districts. She had become a hell-raising female, who established her right to drink in any bar that was reserved exclusively for men, and scorned the dance-houses of the demimonde. If a bartender turned Calamity away, there were plenty of the "boys" who would back her up by saying, "That's Calamity Jane!" Her gruff reply was, "Damn right, it's Calamity!"

While in Abilene, Calamity changed into a feminine figure for a brief period. She claimed to be the innocent daughter of a gambler, Allegheny Dick, and wore her fancy gowns with an elegance that surprised everyone. She was highly regarded for her gentle bearing and admired by the cowhands coming in with droves up from Texas. They gave her the flattering title of "Prairie Queen." This phase, however, was short-lived. Calamity once again donned her masculine attire, saddled her horse and headed for Cheyenne.

Although Calamity Jane was known throughout the West, no

one really knew her. She loved many men, but was never loved in return. Her affection for Wild Bill Hickok lasted throughout her lifetime. Hickok was a Western hero who reputedly killed at least a dozen men in his capacity as a frontier marshal and gambler. He dressed in fancy buckskins with a Stetson hat, wore his hair long and sported a mustache. Hickok knew of Calamity's love for him, but he considered her to be only a friend, and on many occasions a nuisance. When he was shot, she was heartbroken and claimed he had been her lover.

Calamity Jane was a Western legend. Her life has been dramatized by tabloids, newspapers and Dime Novels. Many of the tales are true, most were told by Calamity herself. She drifted throughout the territories, a lonely female misfit who worked at a man's job when it suited her, and as a prostitute when things got tough. Calamity lived a tragic, unconventional life and did not fit into her era. It has been said she was a woman who was born 50 years before her time.

In 1903, at the age of about 51, Calamity Jane died a broken-down old derelict. She was appreciated by all, but respected by few. The citizens of Deadwood buried their legend in style with the largest, gaudiest funeral the town had seen — Calamity Jane was buried beside her unrequited love, Wild Bill Hickok — she would have been pleased!

Timberline

*This Dodge City prostitute was known
throughout the Western Frontier.*

◆ ────────────────────────── ◆

*This mug shot of a suspected prostitute was
taken in Butte, Montana.*

Courtesy of the Wyoming State Museum, Cheyenne, Wyoming

One of Wyoming's "Hog Ranches"

*The hog ranches were a frontier institution.
They could be found along the major thoroughfares
such as the Bozeman Trail and the Cheyenne to
Deadwood Stage Route. These disreputable
establishments raised havoc — not hogs — and catered
to the lowest class of men. They were considered to
be the end of the line for a lady of the night.
This ranch was called Three Mile Ranch.*

Calamity Jane

*This photograph of Calamity Jane shows how
attractive she could be in feminine attire.*

*Calamity Jane wearing her buckskins and boots,
holding the Winchester with which she appeared
many times in books and magazines.*

Wild Bill Hickok

Bill Hickok was the object of Calamity's affections.

AFTER MANY YEARS

After an absence of ten or eleven years, the notorious 'Calamity Jane', who used to figure so prominently in police courts and circles in this city, has again made her appearance in Cheyenne, but evidently in a very dilapidated condition, judging from what is said by those who have seen her. She was first seen here on Wednesday of this week and again on Thursday, but yesterday, so far as could be ascertained, she did not show herself on the streets. 'Calamity' has had a checkered career, and has for years been well known not only here but a (sic) Deadwood, Dak., and many other towns in the far West, and it is only a few months ago that her picture appeared in one of the New York illustrated police papers.

— The Democratic Leader, March 12, 1887

JANE'S JAMBOREE

On Sunday, June 10th, that notorious female, Calamity Jane, greatly rejoiced over her release from durance vile, procured a horse and buggy from Jas. Abney's stable ostensibly to drive to Fort Russell and back. By the time she had reached the Fort, however indulgence in frequent and liberal potations completely befogged her not very clear brain, and she drove right by that place, never drawing rein until she reached the Chug, 50 miles distant. Continuing to imbibe bug-juice at close intervals and in large quantities throughout the night, she woke up the next morning with a vague idea that Fort Russell had been removed, but being still bent on finding it, she drove on, finally sighting Fort Laramie, 90 miles distant. Reaching there she discovered her mistake, but didn't show much disappointment. She turned her horse out to grass, ran the buggy into a corral, and began enjoying life in camp after her usual fashion. When Joe Rankin reached the Fort, several days later, she begged of him not to arrest her, and as he had no authority to do so, he merely took charge of the Abneys outfit, which was brought back to this city Sunday.

— The Cheyenne Daily Leader, June 20, 1876

◆ ────────────────────────────── ◆

*"The only entrance to the crib was a narrow door,
in which was set a small barred window. Occupants
of the den took turns standing behind the bars and
striving to attract the attention of passing men.
When an interested male stopped before the crib, the
harlot displayed the upper part of her body and
cajoled him with seductive cries and motions."*

— The Barbary Coast, by Herbert Asbury

Chapter 8

THE CHINESE SLAVE GIRLS — A LIFE WITHOUT HOPE

Although Abraham Lincoln freed the slaves in 1863, an even more corrupt form of slavery continued to exist in America for another 47 years — White Slavery. In this sordid business, innocent victims ranging from 12 to 19 years in age, were forced into the living hell of prostitution. This vicious bondage upon women lasted until 1910 when the Mann Act was passed by congress, prohibiting the interstate transportation of women for immoral purposes.

The fate of the Chinese slave girls, however, was particularly distressing. These girls were bought for pennies in China, and imported to California to be sold to the highest bidder. The Mann Act, unfortunately, did not help them, as the Chinese slave trade lasted into the 1920s. Many of these frightened girls attempted to flee, but there was no place they could hide and no escape until 1895, when Donaldina Cameron began her crusade on behalf of the little prisoners.

"All of the slave girls in San Francisco, particularly those who occupied the cribs, were shamefully mistreated by their masters. They received no part of their earnings, and most of them never left their dens except for brief periods . . . for failure to please every man who visited them they were lashed with whips and branded with hot irons."[1]

The Chinese girl was considered of little value, even in her own country, for it was her parents who sold her into slavery. She was merely a piece of merchandise to be auctioned to the highest bidder. The girl had no control over her moral or physical condition — a caged animal received more kindness and freedom. Ironically, a

---

[1] **The Barbary Coast**, by Herbert Asbury

Chinese woman named Ah Toy was among the first to procure girls from her own country for California's lucrative slave trade.

Ah Toy arrived in San Francisco about 1849 aboard a China Clipper. Her husband died a few weeks out to sea, and the beautiful woman became the captain's mistress. When she left the Clipper, Ah Toy's pockets were filled with gold and she was wearing the finest silks — the captain had been a generous man.

As the attractive woman strolled toward the Embarcadero, she noticed the attention she was receiving from an excited group of male followers. In China a woman was considered a "worthless female." In San Francisco, however, it appeared the sight of a woman, especially an Oriental, drove the men wild. Ah Toy modestly bowed her head, but her shrewd mind was filled with thoughts of money. If American men became this aroused over the glimpse of a Chinese woman, they would surely pay for the privilege of a closer look.

Although Ah Toy had shared her favors with the captain, she was not at that time a prostitute, merely a satisfactory mistress. Consequently, she decided to open a *look but don't touch show*, and charged as much as the men would pay. Ah Toy rented a two-room building, added a platform in one room and cut round peep holes in the wall. She hired a strong Chinese man to collect one ounce of gold from each eager customer who was willing to pay for a look.

Needless to say, Ah Toy was a great success. When all the peep holes were occupied, she would appear upon the small stage wearing a form-fitting, embroidered silk kimono with a split on both sides from hem to waist. Underneath Ah Toy was totally nude. With each movement of her shapely body, the female-starved men became a little wilder. Soon they were a foot-stomping, howling mass of humanity. The show lasted only a few minutes, but Ah Toy seemed to be on her way to wealth. Her admirers stood waiting in lines over a block long.

Ah Toy's fortune, however, was not to come from the peep show. Her customers began paying with brass nuggets and the Chinese man couldn't tell the real gold from the phony. Ah Toy tried taking the men who cheated her to court, but her case was dismissed. She left her show behind and became the mistress of many men of wealth and prominence. Ah Toy, with their help, went on to become one of the principal and most prosperous dealers in Chinese prostitution. She opened a chain of brothels and cribs throughout California, and was known as San Francisco's first Oriental madam.

Ah Toy imported her own girls from China, where she selected choice females for a very low price. This clever, unscrupulous woman took the inexperienced girls, many as young as 11, and turned them over to the captain and his crew for training. When they arrived in San Francisco, the girls were already knowledgeable prostitutes. They knew the value of a coin and could tell real gold from brass. The girls had learned to say, "pay first," and wore rice powder and rouge upon their once innocent faces.

From 1850 through the turn-of-the-century, thousands of Chinese slaves were brought to America. The majority of the procurers were Orientals seeking a way to make a fat profit. These greedy flesh peddlers purchased pretty, young girls to fill special orders for prosperous merchants, wealthy miners and to sell at private auction.

Many of these children were shipped to San Francisco in large, padded crates like animals. They did not understand English, and had no idea where they were going or what awaited them at the end of a long voyage. Others were sold to "paper" husbands or parents, and brought to America under the pretense of being a wife or daughter. Since small girls in China often married older men, they had no problem with immigration officials. Unfortunately, some Americans willingly looked the other way for a bribe or donation. A few of the older, more beautiful girls were enticed to come to America with the promise of a rich husband or an education, only to be sold into the houses of prostitution.

When the girls first arrived, they were herded into an immense underground cavern, known as the "Queen's Room." For the next few weeks they were under the care of older Chinese women who had survived the ordeal of prostitution. These women taught the girls ways to please men and how to entice them into their cubicles. They learned to say: "China girl very nice! You come inside please, and I make you happy!" Harsh words for little girls to utter.

After the girls were rested and ready for inspection, the buyers were notified of the auction. "When the sale began, the girls were brought in one by one to the block. They were stripped, punched, and prodded and in some cases examined by Chinese physicians . . . A price having been agreed upon for a given girl, the amount in gold or currency, was placed in her outstretched palm. She immediately handed it to the man who had offered her for sale."[1] The girl had been sold.

In order to make the sale legal, the girl was forced to sign a contract that usually said:

For the consideration of _____ paid into my hands on this day, I _____, promise to prostitute my body for the term of _____ years. If, in that time, I am sick one day, two weeks shall be added to my time, and if more than one, my term of prostitution shall be continued an additional month. But if I run away, or escape from the custody of my keepers, then I am to be held a slave for life.

Signed _____

This document was binding. During the female's monthly cycle she would automatically be "ill" for more than one day, unless she was pregnant. Since she was incapacitated at this time, at least one month, therefore, was added to every month of service under the terms of the contract. The Chinese girl was caught on a treadmill which she could never leave, doomed to work until she died of disease, or became too old for the profession. She never received money; the procurer took it from her palm. Since the Chinese girl could not read or write, she signed the contract with her mark, not knowing what was written.

These girls were valuable property. In 1850 they were sold for a few hundred dollars apiece. As their popularity increased, the amount went even higher. During the 1890s, female babies as young as one year began arriving from China to be sold for $100 each. There seemed to be no end to the abuse. What hope could there be for an infant who was trained to be a prostitute before her teens?

---

[1] **The Barbary Coast**, by Herbert Asbury

Following the auction, the girls were placed in either a brothel or a crib. The brothel prostitutes were painted and powdered, sprayed with seductive perfume and dressed in the finest silks. They served the customers drinks and had to entertain any man who requested their services, in whatever manner he chose.

The Oriental girls were very clean. They shaved their bodies daily and took frequent baths. Although 90 percent of them eventually contracted a disease, it was not for lack of cleanliness. Often a girl with special beauty or charm would attract a wealthy client who purchased her for his own exclusive use. When he tired of her, she went back to the brothel or became an independent prostitute. On a few occasions the man would fall in love with the girl and make her his wife. This, however, was rare.

The girls who were sold to the crib owners had an entirely different life. They were sent to work in the rat-infested section of Chinatown and operated out of two small, shabby rooms divided by heavy drapes. In these cramped quarters, as many as six girls plied their trade. They wore embroidered silk blouses, with nothing below. These girls were forced to service the lowest men in the most debased ways imaginable. The average crib girl lasted six years. She was called a "sing song girl," because she had to stand in the doorway of the sordid crib and advertise her charms. Her plaintive voice could be heard throughout the night crying: "Two bittee lookee, flo bittee feelee, six bittee dooee!"

Many of these girls became wild-eyed creatures who were so full of fear and hatred that they would strike out at anyone. In order to calm a girl, her keeper would chain her to the bed and administer narcotics. "Six years was a long time for a girl to live after being placed in a crib, and since she almost invariably began her life of misery and degradation in her early teens, a Chinese prostitute of more than twenty years was a great rarity. Moreover, she was by that time, nothing more than a frightful old hag."[1] When she was of no further use as a prostitute, the girl was placed in a small cell where she had the choice of taking her own life or being murdered.

By 1870 there were several thousand Chinese women and girls in San Francisco. Less than one hundred were respected members of the community. All Chinese, both male and female, were called

[1] **The Barbary Coast**, by Herbert Asbury

"the heathen Chinee," because they maintained the customs of their native land. The men wore braided queues and silk slippers. They were notorious for their opium dens and the little slave girls which were kept carefully locked behind closed doors. "Because of the prejudices of the times, the Chinese girls were not real people to the white community . . . What happened to them was of no real concern. In its lusty frontier character — alive into the 20th century — San Francisco took pride in its sinfulness."[1]

In 1873, the church women began to get involved in Chinatown's vice when they organized the Oriental Board. A Presbyterian mission was built at 920 Sacramento Street, with volunteer rescue workers. In 1895, at the age of 25, a remarkable woman named Donaldina Cameron joined the mission. It was a decision that would change both her life and that of the Chinese girls. Within a short time, Donaldina, who had no previous experience in social work, was running the mission. She and her workers did not wait for the girls to send for help. They went into the alleys and streets to find them. It was more than a crusade for these women, it was a battle against organized prostitution and the freeing of innocent victims.

Donaldina was a lovely, young New Zealand-born Scotch woman with clear blue eyes and a tall, slender build. She was soft-spoken and wore her long, slightly gray hair in a pompadour. Underneath her gentle bearing, however, was a courageous woman who did not know the meaning of the word fear when it came to saving the girls. She soon knew every twisted alley in Chinatown. Donaldina learned who the underground people were, and with the help of the law and sympathetic Chinese, she was almost always successful in her raids upon the Oriental houses of prostitution. Once she was given a clue, Donaldina was off at full speed to run it down — she never gave up.

This exceptional woman was known by two nicknames. She was called "Lo Mo," meaning "Beloved Mother," by the girls who wanted to show the affection they felt for her. On the other hand, the slave dealers and underground called her "Fahn Quai," or "The White Devil," a woman they both feared and despised. These unscrupulous flesh peddlers told the already abused girls that

---

[1] **Women of the West**, by Dorothy Gray

Donaldina was a she-devil who would drink their blood and show them no mercy. But as word of her daring raids spread throughout every miserable brothel and crib in Chinatown, the girls realized that Donaldina was their friend.

Although Lo Mo was a slender woman, she would chop down doors with an ax, and tear away the wood with her own hands to rescue a girl. On one occasion a hunt ended when Donaldina pulled a trap door up and found a girl hidden in a square box between the floor and a false ceiling below. Most of the time the police assisted in these raids, which often led to chases over the rooftops, down twisted alleys and into rat-infested basements. The result being that Lo Mo again rescued yet another prisoner. It was a sordid world of muffled screams, opium fumes and squalor.

The girls themselves eventually began smuggling messages to the mission home through a kind customer. When the rescue took place, the girl would pretend to fight Donaldina in fear. If the raid failed, the girl knew she would be sent off to a mining camp where she would be at the mercy of hundreds of lonely men — Donaldina, however, seldom failed.

All of the girls suffered from years of pain and brutality. They had to learn that kindness still existed and Donaldina, with her faith, strength and love, devoted her life helping the former slaves find a life of dignity. She saw that they received an education and learned responsibility. Many of the girls, who once had no future, entered into matrimony. When this happened, the young man always came to Lo Mo to ask for the girl's hand in marriage. She usually said yes, as well as planned the wedding. The mission had become a place where no girl was turned away, for they were all Donaldina's "children."

In 1928, Yoke Keen, who was rescued by Donaldina, became of the first Chinese women to graduate from Stanford University in Palo Alto, California. When Yoke Keen completed her education, she returned to her native land to help educate her people. Other former slave girls followed Keen, all hoped to better the situation of the burdened women of China. They planned to dedicate their lives as Donaldina had, preventing little girls from being sold for pennies to live a life of slavery.

In 1939 at the age of 70, Donaldina left the mission. She had spent more than 40 years fighting against slavery and prejudice in the Chinese community — it was time for a rest. The beloved Lo Mo retired to a cottage in Palo Alto, where she lived with her two sisters, surrounded by numerous friends and her adopted children. After her sisters passed away, Miss Tien Wu, a former slave and associate, lived with her. On January 4, 1968, one month before her 99th birthday, Donaldina Cameron died of complications from hip surgery.

During her eventful life, many of Donaldina's girls had become her foster children, a few were adopted and all were called her daughters. Lo Mo, and her dedicated helpers, have been credited with the rescue of more than 3,000 Chinese girls. Their courage and commitment to social reform in San Francisco will always be admired and remembered.

The place is loathsome in the extreme. On one side is a shelf four feet wide and about a yard above the dirty floor, upon which there are two old rice mats. There is not the first suggestion of furniture in the room, no table, no chairs or stools, nor any windows. When any of the unfortunate harlots is no longer useful and a Chinese physician passes his opinion that her disease is incurable, she is notified that she must die. Led by night to this hole of a 'hospital,' she is forced within the door and made to lie down upon the shelf. A cup of water, another of boiled rice, and a little metal oil lamp are placed by her side. Those who have immediate charge of the establishment know how long the oil should last, and when the limit is reached they return to the hospital, unbar the door and enter. Generally the woman is dead, either by starvation or from her own hand; but sometimes life is not extinct; the spark remains when the "doctors" enter; yet this makes little difference to them. They come for a corpse and they never go away without it.

San Francisco Chronicle, December 5, 1869

OPIUM DENS

Opium is a powerful narcotic made from a form of poppy grown in the Orient. When properly used it is a valuable medicine. In the hands of the wrong people, however, opium becomes a health hazard that causes addiction and leads to a loss of moral values.

During the 1800s Chinese opium dens could be found throughout the West. Men and women frequented them in order to gain a feeling of euphoria and well being. Most of the customers were entirely dependent upon the drug, and visited these illegal dens of vice on a regular basis.

The opium den usually consisted of tiny, unventilated cubicles, opening off a main hall. Each room had a cot and tables upon which the smoking supplies were laid. The customer placed a prepared pill over a tiny opening in a pipe, then reclined upon one hip on the cot and inhaled the smoke.

When he, or she, drifted off into a rose-colored dream, the pipe was placed on a table. Because the drug often caused nausea, a customer who became ill could lean over the cot and use the bowl placed beneath. It has been said that the term "Hippie," started in the opium dens. Since the customers always leaned upon one hip, they became known as hippies.

Courtesy of the San Francisco Library, San Francisco, California

◆───────────────◆

*Squalid Chinese cribs in
San Francisco's Old Chinatown*

Library of Congress. This photograph was donated by the producers of NOBODY'S GIRLS a docu-drama portraying the lives of minority and subculture women in the American West of 1850-1915. It will appear on public television in the fall of 1994.

◆────────────────────────────────────◆

The Chinese slave girl modestly bows her head as she crosses the street in San Francisco's Old Chinatown. Circa 1855

◆————————————————————◆

*Donaldina Cameron and three of the Chinese girls
she rescued from slavery*

DONALDINA CAMERON

A little white-haired woman, whose gentleness is only equaled by her courage, for thirty-seven years was known as Fahn Quai, the "White Devil" of Chinatown, feared like the plague by its evil doers.

But today she bears another name, "Lo Mo"—Love Mother.

She is Donaldina Cameron, head of the Presbyterian Rescue Mission at 920 Sacramento Street. Under her care the quiet old mission housed 3,000 Chinese girls.

Braving every peril, without thought for her own safety, Miss Cameron invaded the slave marts and the secret hiding places of the traders in human lives whenever word came to her that some helpless girl slave was being held.

More than once she was forced to battle with her own hands, as she beat off the slave traders attempting to wrest rescued girls from her protection.

But those days of thrilling rescues are largely a thing of the past, says Miss Cameron, though there is still some slavery and cause for eternal vigilance on the part of authorities and mission rescue workers.

And so "Fahn Quai," the "White Devil," has become instead, "Lo Mo," beloved mother to the whole community even as she is to the girls she has sheltered, and to their children, for most of them are married comfortably and have families of their own.

Miss Cameron began her work as a fearless, high hearted girl of 20 in the old "days before the fire."

The modern Chinese community is a model compared with the hell-hole of the old days, but even yet there is need in Chinatown, as in other parts of the city, for protection for girls alone in a strange land. Just last week Miss Cameron added two girls to her "family" at the mission. One was taken out of actual slavery and the other, highly educated in Chinese but utterly ignorant of the language and ways of America, was rescued just in time after she had been brought to San Francisco.

San Francisco Chronicle, Monday, October 17, 1932

Timothy Gordon Collection, Missoula, Montana

◆──────────────────────────────◆

Josephine Marcus

*Josephine came to Tombstone as an "actress"
and became the wife of Wyatt Earp.*

Chapter 9

COLORFUL LADIES
OF THE SOUTHWEST

T he Southwestern frontier was a blend of cow towns, ranches and mining communities. Its men and women were a hard - bitten breed who drifted throughout the West in search of adventure and wealth. Due to the often desolate living conditions, and high mortality rate, the citizens were less likely to criticize others than those who lived in the more urban areas. Most communities of the Southwest accepted the "soiled doves" as a part of their society.

When John Clum was elected Mayor of Tombstone, Arizona in 1881, the houses of prostitution, formerly confined to a red light district, were allowed to spread into the residential community. He felt this gave the town a friendly atmosphere. It also helped eliminate the shooting and fighting that frequently took place on "Whiskey Row," along Allen and Fremont Streets.

Tombstone was a lusty, bawdy camp - type town with a boot hill that was frequently used. Notorious gunslingers like Doc Holliday, the "Clanton Gang" and the Earp brothers; Wyatt, Virgil and Morgan strolled along the dusty streets. Its men were devoid of fear and fast on the draw. The women, independent and used to living with violence, were known by names like "Irish Mag," "Crazy Horse Lil" and "Dutch Annie." "Big Nose Kate," however, was the most notorious, for she was the mistress of the elusive Doc Holliday.

Kate's real name was Mary Katherine Horony. She was born November 7, 1850 in Budapest, Hungary. The family immigrated to Davenport, Iowa, and a few years later Kate was left an orphan. She ran away from a foster home at the age of 18, and became a Dodge City dance hall girl.

Kate met Doc Holliday 11 years later, while she was working as a dance hall prostitute in Fort Griffin, Texas. Doc had cut a man's throat during a game of poker, and was being held prisoner in a hotel room. A mob had gathered, and there was talk of a lynching. Kate distracted the men by setting fire to an adjacent livery stable. When the mob rushed to extinguish the flames, she ran into the hotel and threatened the sheriff with a pair of Colt .45s. When Doc was released, the couple galloped off to Dodge City.

Although Doc was a well - educated gentleman gambler from the South, and Kate an illiterate soiled dove, this unlikely pair formed a strong bond that lasted throughout Doc's lifetime. While he was cool and refined, Kate was known for her fast temper and fierce independence. She was an attractive woman with a voluptuous body who was given the sobriquet of "Big Nose Kate," due to a prominent nose.

When Doc and Kate arrived in Dodge City, they decided it was time to become respectable citizens. Doc hung up his shingle as a dentist and Kate gave up her profession. This, however, didn't last long — both missed their former lives. Kate left Doc for the excitement of the saloons with their lusty men, and Doc returned to the gaming tables.

A year later they were back together in Colorado, where Doc became involved in a shooting incident. Although he was known for his fast draw, it must be remembered that Doc never intentionally looked for a fight. He was a level - headed professional gambler who considered the odds carefully before reaching for his gun.

Following the shooting, the couple left Colorado and were seen in various places of the West. They eventually drifted into Tombstone. Doc and the Earp brothers were good friends and the gaming houses were filled with men who had become wealthy from the rich silver strike. With Doc back at the tables, Kate pursued her profession as a prostitute.

A few weeks later "Rowdy Kate," an old friend of Big Nose Kate, appeared in Tombstone, and the ladies decided to open the town's first brothel. They erected a large tent, ordered barrels of cheap whiskey and hired several "working girls." The establishment wasn't fancy, but the men flocked in from all directions. The primary rule of the house was never let a man leave while there was money in his pocket — and the girls didn't. Although the brothel was successful, the business arrangement didn't last long. The women began to fight and Big Nose Kate started drinking so much that Rowdy Kate had to take over management. Shortly thereafter other brothels began opening and Rowdy Kate moved on.

Big Nose Kate continued to drink, and she often became an abusive drunk. She and Doc constantly argued and Kate, in a fit of anger, moved to Globe, Arizona. But she could never stay away from Doc long, and frequently returned to Tombstone to visit him. On October 26, 1881, she was in Doc's room at Fly's Boarding House when the famous fight at the O.K. Corral occurred. Kate was the only witness to the event that became a part of Western history. From her window she saw the Earps and Holliday face Tom and Frank McLaury, Ike and Billy Clanton, and Billy Claibourne in the vacant lot next to the corral. While watching, Kate saw her lover calmly walk away alive from the bloody scene.

Obviously this was the end for Kate, as she had seen enough bloodshed. She returned to Globe and it is believed she never saw Doc again. He continued to live a violent life and was admired throughout the West for his lack of fear and fast guns. Doc was a man's man who stood up for his rights, even if it meant death — and it ultimately did! Doc Holliday met his fate in 1887.

The following year, Kate married a blacksmith in Arizona; she settled down to become a faithful wife and to cook for the miners. When the blacksmith began spending her money on his alcohol, Kate moved on, working at various trades. She eventually became a housekeeper for a wealthy gentleman and remained with him until his death 29 years later. In 1931, Kate was admitted to the "Arizona Pioneer Home," where she died in 1940. Kate lived to be 90 years old.

———————◆———————

During Tombstone's notorious past it was the wildest place in the West and known as "the town too tough to die." Despite the reputation, it was not just another haunt for desperados; Tombstone was one of the famous mining camps with the richest silver mines of the day. Its brothels were among the finest.

"Blonde Marie," was one of the celebrated ladies. She was a beautiful French woman and the madam of Tombstone's first syndicated brothel. Her elegant establishment was furnished with gilt mirrors, marble tables and the fanciest bedrooms in town. The house was a class-act filled with charming French women. Marie entertained only the wealthiest gentlemen. Her supply of merchandise was frequently exchanged — there were always fresh, new faces. Marie saved her money and returned to Paris, where she lived a life of luxury. Her replacement was a woman known as Madame Moustache, a gambling lady who was familiar throughout the West. History has not been kind to this woman, whose name was Eleanora Dumont. At one time she had owned several gambling houses and was famous for her skill with the cards and her new stylish establishments. It was said she had the ability to mine gold without digging for it. Many miners claimed they would rather lose their money to Madame than to win with somebody else.

In later years, when she had lost her youth, Eleanora turned to prostitution. The slight growth that once was fuzz upon her upper lip, turned dark and earned her the sobriquet of Madame Moustache. Eleanora, however, had not lost her sparkling personality and sense of humor. She was a popular madam and respected by both her girls and the customers. Under her management the brothel showed a marked increase in profits

When Madame Moustache left Tombstone, she wandered through the camps and mining towns, growing older and less confident. Gamblers and bartenders who had known her in better times, treated her with respect, but they could not give Eleanora back her youth and skill with the cards. The unfortunate lady eventually ended up in Bodie, one of the roughest mining towns in the West. On September 8, 1897, her dead body was found a mile out of town. Beside it lay a bottle of poison — Madame Eleanora Dumont, like many other ladies, had found her escape in suicide.

All the prostitutes of Tombstone, from the cribs to the brothels, had to have a medical certificate stating they had visited the local physician, Dr. Goodfellow. Each week he checked the ladies to be sure they were free of disease. If a girl was found to be infected, she couldn't pursue her profession until the doctor said she had been treated and cured. These ladies of negotiable virtue also had to pay for a business license. The funds generated were used as revenue for the schools.

The scarlet ladies of Tombstone, like the rest of the ladies of the West, were the first to assist in time of need. They cared for the injured, opened their houses for the ill and comforted the dying. When the town needed a house of worship, the Episcopal Church was built with money donated by gamblers, saloon - keepers and the houses of ill repute.

Although the West was noted for its many theatres, only Tombstone could boast of The Bird Cage. In his book, Legendary Characters of Southeast Arizona, Ben T. Traywick describes the place of entertainment as follows:

> *The building has one and a half stories, two main rooms — a saloon and theatre section. Balconies, divided into boxes, run down the length of both sides. Percentage girls distributed drinks to these suspended boxes singing as they served — hence the name Bird Cage. Stage lighting is accomplished by a gas system. Scenery and the back-drops are built and painted by the actors as they need them.*

The theatre offered a variety of entertainment — most of it bawdy. "The tastes of its patrons were low and merry and the management sought to oblige."[1] Through the years The Bird Cage constantly attempted to become respectable, but it seldom succeeded. Even a free "Ladies Night" rarely interested the proper women of Tombstone. When the solid citizens did merge with the colorful customers there was usually a disaster. It seemed The Bird Cage Theatre was doomed to entertain an audience of miners, cowboys and fancy ladies. This notorious theatre became the inspiration for the song, *She Was Only A Bird In A Gilded Cage.* Its words — "Her beauty she sold for an old man's gold"— aptly described the ladies who worked there.

When the theatre closed in 1883 it went through a series of owners. In 1886, Joe and Minnie Bignon bought and refurbished The Bird Cage, and reopened it as the Elite Theatre. The Bignons fared better, for they offered top - rate entertainment. While under

---

[1] **The American West**, by Lucius Beebe

their ownership, Joe's wife, who was called "Big Minnie," often performed. On these occasions she was billed as: "Big Minnie" — six feet tall and 230 pounds of loveliness in pink tights.[1] What the playbill didn't say, however, was that Minnie frequently filled in as their bouncer.

As Tombstone began its decline, a few of the women exchanged their profession for respectability. Crazy Horse Lil left town and disappeared. Irish Mag loaned money to a prospector and ended up with a fortune and Dutch Annie died a heroine, due to her many good deeds. When the boom of Tombstone ended, Joe and Minnie Bignon left town, but Tombstone itself never faded — it lives on today as it did in the past — still too tough to die!

———————◆———————

In the mid-1800s, the shortage of women in the cow towns and scattered homesteads of the Texas Panhandle, was critical. Lonely cowboys sat around their campfires, singing songs of unrequited love, while overworked homesteaders attempted to establish a home. Marriageable women were so scarce that a tattooed, female snake charmer, in the circus of P. T. Barnum, married a respected citizen, while a squatter, with eight daughters, was welcomed into the community.

In Canadian, one of the towns along the Canadian River, men arrived by the hundreds to set up businesses for the railroad. Entrepreneurs built saloons and brought in fancy ladies to entertain them. The ladies, however, seldom remained in the saloons, for the eager men swept them off their feet and carried them away for a marriage license.

In Tascosa, which was originally named Otascosa, shacks, tents, dugouts and an occasional log cabin were erected. The citizens of Tascosa thought the railroad was coming, and they wanted their town ready to reap the harvest from the heavy trade it would bring. Tascosa had the usual amount of saloons, dance halls and soiled doves clustered among the small dwellings that were spread throughout the town. On Saturday nights the locals were often treated to a visit from their favorite desperado, Billy the Kid. Whenever he was in the area, The Kid stopped to pay his respects.

The sight of a soiled dove in Tascosa was not offensive; they

[1] **Legendary Characters of Southeast Arizona**, by Ben T. Traywick

were not set apart in a designated area. The dance hall girls and prostitutes were included in the community. Their children went to school and played with the other children, without a hint of discrimination. No one in Tascosa asked questions, for it was not that kind of a town. Marriage was preferable, but not necessary.

The town was filled with colorful characters. "Shorty" Delaine was a clerk in one of the stores and the town's practical joker. The fancy ladies had names like "Rocking Chair Emma," "Mustang Mae" and "Santa Fe Mol." Emma lived in a little log cabin with bright curtains at the windows and a vegetable patch out back. Every day she sat in her rocking chair, occasionally taking a nip from the jug of whiskey she kept by her side. When a gentleman came to call, Emma took care of his needs and returned to her rocking chair and her jug. Mustang Mae was a wild filly and swore like a seasoned bullwhacker and Santa Fe Mol was a traveling woman who drifted in and out of town.

Mickey McCormick and his girl Frenchy, were a step apart from the rest. "Mickey was a small Irish gambler and livery - stable operator. Frenchy was a dance - hall girl who had run away from a convent in Louisiana, migrated by easy steps to St. Louis, Dodge City, then to Mobeetei, where, when she was eighteen years of age, McCormick had seen her. It was love at first sight, and he had brought her to Tascosa with him."[1]

Frenchy was a charming young woman with a gentle smile and sparkling personality. She and Mickey were deeply in love and lived together in a cottage he built down by the creek. Although she had been a soiled dove, Frenchy had left that part of her life behind and was content to work in her flower garden and take care of her man.

Tascosa was known as a wild gambling and drinking town, with a lack of law and order. The people lived independently and resented any interference from the outside. When word spread through town that a sheriff would soon be appointed, Mickey knew the clergy would not be far behind. Until then he and Frenchy had not needed a marriage license, but with the arrival of "respectable" women, it became a necessity. Mickey did not want anyone to call Frenchy a soiled dove, for she was the most important person in his

[1] **Maverick Town: The Story of Old Tascosa**, by John L. McCarty

life. They were married first by a justice of the peace and then in the Catholic Church.

Theirs was a very special marriage, filled with romance and respect. Mickey visited the gaming house nightly, and when Lady Luck failed to smile upon him he sent for Frenchy. She always brought a cheery smile and the cards would come his way. Each day Frenchy loved her little Irish gambler just a little bit more than the day before.

When Mickey died in 1912, a part of Frenchy died too; there could never be another man in her life. She continued to live alone in the house by the creek, tending her flower garden and visiting Mickey's grave.

The railroad never came to Tascosa and the town slowly began to disappear. One by one the citizens left, and soon only Frenchy and 15 residents remained. Frenchy swore she would never leave Mickey as long as she lived, and she never did. When she died in 1941, no one knew how old Frenchy was, for she had never shared her past. She was buried beside Mickey. Frenchy McCormick will always be remembered as the last of Tascosa's survivors. She had been alone for almost a quarter of a century and was referred to as one of the "Girls of the Golden West."

Not all of the communities in the Panhandle were as laid back as Tascosa. In Amarillo, the soiled doves were restricted to the red light district. Although many of these ladies had a fine reputation with the merchants and the bankers, they were not accepted by society. Unlike Tascosa, their children weren't welcome to attend school or play with the offspring of the proper women. They were either sent away to live with relatives or placed in boarding homes.

One of the admired madams of the early west operated her business in Amarillo. She was a beautiful woman, with dark eyes and thick, raven hair who was known as Ella Hill. Her dance hall and brothel were the largest in the Panhandle and very popular. The girls employed there were a cut above the average and known for their beauty and decency; there were no alcoholics or drug users in Ella's place.

No one is quite sure of Ella's past, but everyone knew she had two daughters she dearly loved. It was said that Ella's husband had abandoned her, leaving Ella to raise the two little girls alone. She had tried to take care of them by working as a laundress, then became a waitress. Neither of these jobs provided enough money to support her children, so she left them with a respected family and, like so many women before her, turned to prostitution.

Ella often said her first job was with a kind madam in a high - class brothel. It was hard work for a woman who had once been respected, however, there were two daughters to be raised. Ella learned the profession and was soon a sought - after prostitute. Her employer provided a fine example for Ella to follow, for she was an honest woman and always considerate of her girls.

Ella worked hard and saved her money. After a few years, she left her job and opened her first business. It was small and successful, and she slowly moved up to larger houses, always maintaining a reputation for honesty and integrity. When Ella moved to Amarillo, she was already a highly regarded madam and established in the West.

Her house was noted for its well - mannered young women and clean, comfortable rooms. She did not allow profanity or excessive drinking, and no one took advantage of the customers. A man's money was as safe in his pockets there as it would have been in his pockets in his own home. Ella's clients were wealthy and they trusted her. Many of them would go on a spree and stay at her house for two or three days; drinking, gambling and enjoying the company of the girls. When they left, Ella handed them a carefully prepared bill, listing all of the expenses. Some of the well-to-do ranchers would just hand their money over to Ella upon arrival, knowing they would receive the correct amount when they left, and that their reputation was intact.

When the town needed a church, Ella contributed a considerable amount of her money from what was considered a life of sin. Since the respectable citizens gladly accepted the madam's money, she felt her ladies should be welcome to visit the new place of worship. Her concern for the girls' souls was so great that she required her employees to accompany her to church. Every Sunday morning the madam and her prostitutes, dressed in modest gowns, appeared among the members of the congregation in the house of the Lord. If the town felt any resentment toward Ella and her girls, they kept it to themselves.

As the years passed, Ella continued to run her establishment, maintaining what was considered the finest brothel in the Southwest. When she felt it was time to retire, Ella sold her home and moved to Wichita, Kansas, where she opened a laundry. Ella's new business was unique, for she employed only former prostitutes. These women, who had been forgotten by society, would take the soiled linen to their homes, launder it and bring the parcels back to Ella. Although it was menial work, it made the women feel they earned their money by doing an honorable service.

When Ella died, her remains where shipped to Amarillo to be buried. She did not have a large funeral, only a few of her former friends and customers came to pay their respects. Sadly, her two daughters were not counted among those attending. Throughout her life Ella had constantly visited her daughters. They never knew what kind of work their mother did, and they grew into womanhood believing she was a housekeeper for a wealthy Western rancher. Both girls married prominent men and went on to raise respectable families. Ella would not have wanted them to attend her last rites, it would have ruined all that she had spent her life working for. In her daughters' eyes, she was not a soiled dove.

Courtesy of the Arizona Historical Society, Tucson, Arizona

"*Rowdy Kate*"

Courtesy of the Arizona Historical Society, Tucson, Arizona

The Bird Cage Theatre

MASQUERADE BALL

Monday night last a bal masque was given at the Bird Cage under the auspices of its manager, Billy Hutchinson. It was an advent in town that couldn't be missed, as it gave an opportunity to deacons and other religious people to get a peep into the inner workings of the Cage, which I am assured was taken advantage of by a large number, as several in the crowd were pointed out and their names given me, but for the sake of the town's morals I will not expose them, as it would kick up a mess in society circles and add fuel to the collected stock of scandal - mongers. For my part, I do not see why, if he wants to, a deacon has not as good right to hold a lovely Miss upon his knees and fire wine into her as anyone. As the ball advanced and diversion grew interesting, staid old citizens, who never before were seen to frequent like places, became hilarious, under the combined pressure of madams and so much feminine loveliness exposed to them... Like amusements were indulged in til old Sol rose in all his majestic glory in the early morn when the godly as ungodly took themselves away to dream of Bird Cages and canaries.

— The Arizona Star, October 22, 1882

"Big Minnie"

She was billed as:
"Big Minnie"— six feet tall
and 230 pounds of
loveliness in pink tights.

May Davenport

May arrived in Tombstone
with a traveling carnival
and remained to become
a prostitute.

Courtesy of the Arizona Historical Society, Tucson, Arizona

In 1882, the New York Times called the Bird Cage Theatre America's most notorious and bawdiest honky-tonk.

Courtesy of the Panhandle-Plains Historical Museum, Canyon, Texas

◆ ———————————— ◆

Mickey McCormick

Courtesy of the Panhandle-Plains Historical Museum, Canyon, Texas

◆ ————————————————— ◆

Frenchy McCormick

GLOSSARY

Bagnio - A synonym for a house of prostitution.

"Boarding House" - A term used by Western madams to infer that their brothels were respectable. The women who worked in these establishments usually paid board and room, hence the term "Boarding House".

Bordello - A synonym for a house of prostitution.

Brothel - A house of prostitution.

"Company, ladies" - These words, accompanied by the tinkle of a bell, let the prostitutes know that the customers had arrived and it was time to go to work.

Courtesan (Courtezan) - A euphemistic term for a high-class prostitute who sold her sexual favors to a man of wealth and prominence for money or social gain. In 17th century Europe, the word courtesan was used to describe a woman who was the mistress of a king or royalty. The term "Courtezan" started in France.

Crib - A small dwelling in which a prostitute sold sexual favors. Most of the women also lived in their cribs.

Demimonde - A class of women who have lost their reputation due to their behavior. A member of the Demimonde would be a woman who had joined the sisterhood of prostitution.

Fair but Frail - A synonym for a prostitute.

"Girls" - A polite term for prostitutes.

Hog Ranch - A frontier term for a low-class house of prostitution.

"House" - Brothel

Hurdy-Gurdy - A form of mechanical hand organ with strings, keys and wooden wheels that produced music when the handle was turned. It was first used in Europe and became a popular musical instrument in America during the 1800s.

Hurdy-Gurdy Girl or "Hurdy" - A dancer in a hurdy-gurdy house, or one who traveled with a musical company which offered hurdy-gurdy music.

Lady of Easy Virtue - A synonym for a prostitute.

Lady of the Evening - Same as above.

Lady of the Night - Same as above.

Madam - Either the manager or owner of a brothel.

GLOSSARY

Mistress - The illicit ladylove of a married man, or a woman who lived with a man over a period of time for money or material gain.

"Mother" - A term often referring to a kind madam who was loved by her girls.

Painted Lady - A synonym for a prostitute. "Proper" women did not wear makeup.

Parlor House - An elite brothel.

Pimp - A man who makes his living procuring for a prostitute and lives off her income.

Procurer - A person who makes a living providing women for sexual purposes.

Prostitute - A woman who offers her body for hire for the purpose of sexual favors or intercourse.

"Old-timer" - A prostitute who has been in the same brothel for a long period of time, or who is an older, more experienced woman.

Red Light District - A designated section of a town or city where houses of prostitution are found.

Skid Road - A logging term which once meant a trail of greased skids used by ox teams to haul logs to the sawmills. A "Skid Road" in any logging or sawmill town became the term for the district containing brothels and saloons which catered to the needs of loggers and lumbermen.

Soiled Dove - A synonym for a prostitute.

Streetwalker - A prostitute who solicits sex on the streets.

Tenderloin - A synonym for a red light district. It originated in New York and referred to a section of the city where vice and police corruption were common.

White Slavery - The interstate transportation of young women for immoral purposes.

BIBLIOGRAPHY ~ PRIMARY SOURCES

Chapter 1. Silk Stockings and Fancy Lingerie
Books: *Adler, Polly, A House Is Not A Home*, 1953; Bernhart, Jacqueline Baker, *The Fair But Frail: Prostitution in San Francisco 1849-1900*, 1986; Butler, Anne M., Daughters of Joy, Sisters of Misery: *Prostitution in the American West 1865-1900*, 1987; Richardson, Albert, Beyond *The Mississippi*, 1869; Persea Books, *Madeleine, An Autobiography*, Reprint, 1986.

Chapter 2. It Happened on Holladay Street
Books: Asbury, Herbert, *The Barbary Coast*, 1933; Bancroft, Caroline, *Six Racy Madams of Colorado*, 1965; Glasscock, C. B., *Lucky Baldwin*; Parkhill, Forbes, *The Wildest of The West*, 1951. Newspapers: *Denver Daily Times*, September 4, 1886; *Rocky Mountain News*, April 28, 1898; *Denver Republic*, May 4, 1889. Special Articles: Western History Department, Denver Public Library and The Colorado Historical Society, Denver, Colorado.

Chapter 3. Working Girls
Books: Adler, Polly, *A House Is Not A Home*, 1953; Asbury, Herbert, *The Barbary Coast*, 1933; Butler, Anne M., *Daughters of Joy, Sisters of Misery: Prostitution in the American West 1865-1900*, 1987; Lake, Stuart, *Wyatt Earp: Frontier Marshall*, 1931; Snell, Joseph W., *Painted Ladies of the Cowboy Frontier*, 1965. Newspapers: *Denver Times*, January 24, 1891; *Rocky Mountain News*, July 7, 1876. Dissertation: David Courtright, Rice University, 1979.

Chapter 4. The Love Story of Lottie Johl
Books: Cain, Ella M., *The Story of Bodie*, 1956; Chalfant Press, Bishop, California, Reprint, *The Ghost Town of Bodie*, 1977. Periodicals: Kaltenbach, Peter J., "What Bodie Did To Lottie Johl", *True West*, December 1975. Documents: Mono County.

Chapter 5. The Entrepreneurs
Books: Drago, Harry Sinclair, *Notorious Ladies of the Frontier*, 1969; Holdenridge, Helen, *Mammy Pleasant*, 1950; Morgan, Murray, *Skid Road: An Informal Portrait of Seattle*, 1951; Speidel, William C., *Doc Maynard: The Man Who Invented Seattle*, 1978. Newspapers: *Helena Daily Independent*, October 26, 1899; *San Francisco Examiner*, October 13, 1895; *San Francisco Chronicle*, July 9, 1899. Journals: Meyers, Rex C., "An Inning For Sin", *The Montana Magazine*, 1987; Petrik, Paula, "Capitalists With Rooms: Prostitution in Helena, Montana, 1865-1900", *Montana* (3) 1981. Special Information: Charles V. Mutschler, Assistant Archivist, Eastern Washington University, Cheney, Washington.

BIBLIOGRAPHY ~ PRIMARY SOURCES

Chapter 6. Molly b'Dam
Books: Brainard, Wendell, *Golden History Tales From Idaho's Mining Districts*, Mellon, Deborah, *The Legend of Molly b' Dam'*, 1989; Stoll, William T., *Silver Strike*, 1932. Newspapers: *Kellogg Evening News*, August 12, 1963; The Wallace Miner, December 16, 1937; *Kellogg Evening News*, December 22, 1972. Dissertation: Kozisek, Jim, "Molly b' Dam", the University of Idaho, December, 1982.

Chapter 7. A Little Affection, Please
Books: Aikman, Duncan, *Calamity Jane and Other Wildcats*, 1927; Butler, Anne M., *Daughters of Joy, Sisters of Misery: Prostitutes in the American West, 1865- 1900*, 1987; Horan, James D., *Desperate Women*, 1953; McClernan, John B., *Slade's Wells Fargo Colt*, 1977; Towles, Virginia Rowe, *Vigilante Woman*, 1966; Vestal, Stanley, *Queen of the Cowtowns: Dodge City*, 1952; Newspapers: *Rocky Mountain News*, July 7, 1876; *Butte Daily Miner*, August 28, 1879; *Territorial Enterprise* (Virginia City, Nevada), June 7, 1877; *Record-Times* (Wheatland, Wyoming), June 23, 1966; *Torrington Telegram* (Wyoming), February 10, 1982; *Casper Star Tribune* (Wyoming), November 4, 1969. Journals: *The Montana Magazine of History*, January, 1953.

Chapter 8. The Chinese Slave Girls - A Life Without Hope
Books: Asbury, Herbert, *The Barbary Coast*, 1933; Dobie, Charles C., *San Francisco's Chinatown*, 1936; Wilson, Carol, *China Quest: Life Adventures of Donaldina Cameron*, 1931. Journals: Harrison, John H., "Lookee, Lookee, No Touchee", *Real West Magazine*, January, 1973; Hirate, Lucy Cheng, "Free, Indentured, Enslaved: Chinese Prostitution in Nineteenth Century America", Signs 5, 1979. Newspapers: *The San Francisco Chronicle*, October 17, 1932; *The San Francisco Chronicle*, December 5, 1869.

Chapter 9. Colorful Ladies of the Southwest
Books: Butler, Anne M., *Daughters of Joy, Sisters of Misery: Prostitution in the American West, 1865-1900*, 1987; Hamlin, James, *The Flamboyant Judge*, 1972; McCarty, John, *Maverick Town: The Story of Old Tascosa*, 1988; Snell, Joseph, *Painted Ladies of the Cowtown Frontier*, 1965; Traywick, Ben T., *Helles Belles*, 1993; Traywick, Ben T., *Legendary Characters of Southwest Arizona*, 1992. Newspapers: *Arizona Star*, October 22, 1882; The Tascosa Pioneer, February 9, 1887.

BIBLIOGRAPHY

Adler, *Polly, A House Is Not A Home*, 1953

Aikman, Duncan, *Calamity Jane and Other Wildcats*, 1927

Asbury, Herbert, *The Barbary Coast*, 1933, Reprint, 1947

Bancroft, Caroline, *Six Racy Madams of Colorado*, 1965

Bernhart, Jacqueline Baker, *The Fair But Frail: Prostitution in San Francisco, 1849-1900*, 1986

Brainard, Wendell, *Golden Tales From Idaho's Mining District*

Brodsky, Annette, *The Female Offender*, 1965

Bullough, Vern and Bullough, Bonnie, *Prostitution: an Illustrated Social History*, 1978

Butler, Anne M., *Daughters of Joy, Sisters of Misery: Prostitution in the American West, 1865-1900*, 1987

Cain, Ella, *The Story of Bodie*, 1956

Chalfant Press, *The Ghost Town of Bodie*, Reprint, 1977

Dkystra, Robert, *The Cattle Towns*, 1973

Dobie, Charles C., *San Francisco's Chinatown*, 1936

Drago, Harry Sinclair, *Notorious Ladies of the Frontier*, 1969

Glassock, C. B., *Lucky Baldwin*, 1933

Goldman, Marion S., *Gold Diggers and Silver Miners: Prostitution and Social Life on the Comstock Lode*, 1981

Gray, Dorothy, *Women of the West*, 1987

Hamlin, James, *The Flamboyant Judge*, 1972

Holdenridge, Helen, *Mammy Pleasant*, 1950

Horan, James D., *Desperate Women*, 1953

Lake, Stuart, *Wyatt Earp: Frontier Marshall*, 1931

McCarty, John, *Maverick Town: The Story of Old Tascosa*, 1988

McClernan, John B., *Slade's Wells Fargo Colt*, 1977

McCool, Grace, *Gunsmoke: The True Story of Old Tombstone*, 1990

BIBLIOGRAPHY

McHugh, Paul, *Prostitution and Victorian Social Reform*,   1980

Mellon, Deborah, *The Legend of Molly b' Dam'* ,   1989

Morgan, Murray, *Skid Road: An Informal Portrait of Seattle,   1951*

Parkhill, Forbes, *The Wildest of the West,   1951*

Persea Books, *Madeleine, an Autobiography*,   Reprint, 1986

Richardson, Albert, *Beyond the Mississippi,   1869*

Rosen, Ruth, *The Sisterhood: Prostitution in America 1900-1918,*   1982

Ross, Nancy Wilson, *Westward the Women,   1944*

Speidel, William C., *Doc Maynard: The Man Who Invented Seattle,*   1978

Snell, Joseph W., *Painted Ladies of the Cowboy Frontier,   1965*

Stoll, William T., *Silver Strike,   1932*

Towle, Virginia Rowe, *Vigilante Woman,   1966*

Traywick, Ben T., *Helles Belles,   1993*

Traywick, Ben T., *Legendary Characters of Southwest Arizona,   1992*

Vestal, Stanley, *Queen of Cowtowns: Dodge City,   1952*

JOURNALS, MAGAZINES AND DISSERTATIONS:

Harrison, John H., "Lookee, Lookee, No Touchee," *Real West Magazine*, January, 1973

Hirate, Lucie Cheng, "Free, Indentured, Enslaved: Chinese Prostitution in Nineteenth Century America," *Signs 5*, 1979

Kaltenback, Peter, "What Bodie Did To Lottie Johl," *True West Magazine*, December, 1975

Koziski, Jim, "Molly b' Damn" Dissertaton, University of Idaho, 1981

Meyers, Rex C., "An Inning For Sin," *The Montana Magazine*, 1987

Petrik, Paula, "Capitalists With Rooms: Prostitution in Helena, Montana 1865-1900, Montana (3), 1981

West, Elliot, "Scarlet West: the Oldest Profession in the Trans-Mississipi, Montana (1), 1981

NEWSPAPERS:

Alta California

Arizona Star

Arizona Weekly Citizen

Butte Daily Miner

California Courier

Casper Star Tribune (Wyoming)

Denver Daily Times

Denver Republic

Gold Hill News (Nevada)

Helena Daily Independent

Kellogg Evening News (Idaho)

Record Times (Wyoming)

Rocky Mountain News (Colorado)

San Francisco Chronicle

San Francisco Examiner

The Tascosa Pioneer (Texas)

Territorial Enterprise (Nevada)

Torrington Telegraph (Wyoming)

The Wallace Miner (Idaho)

Order these exciting books, by Western author Anne Seagraves, Today!

HIGH-SPIRITED WOMEN OF THE WEST The West is alive! Filled with all the action normally found only in hard-boiled fiction, these true stories bring to life the women who helped shape history. With courage and determination, they left conventional roles behind, becoming America's early feminists. Demanding acceptance on their terms, these high-spirited women proudly took their place in history beside men of the untamed West. Includes stories of Jessie Benton Fromont, Sara Winnemucca, Belle Star, Abigail Duniway and Helen Wiser, the woman who founded Las Vegas.—Autographed—176 pages, illustrated $11.95

WOMEN WHO CHARMED THE WEST These revealing stories tell of the lives and often shocking love affairs of yesterday's leading ladies. Extolled for their beauty and avoiding disgrace by virtue of their charm, these famous actresses livened up an otherwise drab existence as they entertained the Early West. Lillian Russell and Lillie Langtry were glamorous and indiscreet; Adah Issacs Menken, a Victorian rebel, and the delightful Annie Oakley, won the heart of America. This book contains many portraits from famous collections and articles from Annie Oakley's personal scrapbook.—Autographed—176 pages, illustrated $11.95

WOMEN OF THE SIERRA This book offers a touching account of the lives of women achievers from the mid-1800's through the turn-of-the-century. These courageous ladies fought for independence in the male-dominated West, and opened the doors for others to follow. Each woman left her imprint in the Sierra, all were important to the West. Stories include Nevada's first woman doctor, the hanging of Juanita, stage driver Charlotte "Charley" Parkhurst, and Lotta Crabtree, the child "fairy star" of the Sierra. Many of the histories and photos came from the descendents of the women in this heart-warming book.—Autographed—176 pages, illustrated $11.95

DAUGHTERS OF THE WEST ROUGH, TOUGH, AND IN SKIRTS! Gun-toting ladies capture the feminine side of the west. Stories include "Mustang Jane," who ruled the range with her six shooters, Kittie Wilkins, "The Queen of Diamonds," stagedriver Delia Haskett and the strange saga of "Mountain Charley." —Autographed—176 pages, illustrated $11.95

ROSES OF THE WEST Roses captures the spirit of the West with fascinating stories of unforgettable women. Like the Western rose, these women were strong and independent as they opened the doors for others to follow. —Autographed—176 pages, illustrated $11.95

To order your own autographed book(s), send a check for $11.95 for each separate title. Postage will be paid by the publisher. Residents of Idaho, please add 5% sales tax.

Mail to: Wesanne Publications
P.O. Box 428
Hayden, Idaho 83835

Thank you for your order!